live
Boldly

More Praise for *Live Boldly* and Mary Anne Radmacher

"Mary Anne has power in her words. Whether you're looking for a refresher course to remind you to stay on the path of doing the right thing, or you're looking for direction on how to take the first step, *pick up this book and read it.*"
—Troy McClain, international motivational speaker,
award-winning television host, and official spokesperson
for the 2009 Special Olympics World Winter Games

"Mary Anne has the ability to communicate true wisdom, practical motivation, and fun in a simple yet profound way. This is her true genius."
—Connie Fails

"With a patchwork of qualities to embolden your life, Mary Anne Radmacher generously brings her stories and experiences alive on the page. Her words are simple and easy to grasp, woven together in an easy-to-understand way. Read her book for guidance and attention towards a more vivid, colorful, and bold life."
—Beth Miller, author of *The Woman's Book of Resilience*

"Whenever the storm clouds of my own world appear overwhelming, I turn to Mary Anne's words for a reminder that everything good is possible in its own way and its own time. I love the way Mary Anne tells a story. Turn to the Compassion chapter of *Live Boldly*. It drips like honey off her pen: I smell the smells, feel the fear, and smile at the incoherent way life runs us in circles while inscribing the real lessons in a corner of the margin."
—Jonathan Huie, facilitator of Collaborative Group Planning

"*Live Boldly* offers the tools we need to move beyond merely surviving each day to living more fully and deliberately."
—Christine Witt-Trzcinski, president of Brush Dance, Inc.

"I often find myself too busy or too disorganized to know where to start on this exciting life I've imagined. After reading Mary Anne's new book, I believed I could live a full, invigorated life. The book is a breath of fresh air when you most need it."
—Gee Gee Rosell, owner of Buxton Village Books

"Thirty-five small bits of wisdom. Thirty-five uh-huh-head-nodding-moments. Whether you take it in all at once, or read it in small bites, if you're ready to live boldly this is the book to read!"
—Sue Opeka, owner of The Present Moment

"Beginning with the affirmation that living boldly does not mean living loudly, Mary Anne walks us through a tapestry of life values, managing to simplify the complex while adding nuance to the commonplace. Her toolbox is a palette of sensory approaches—writing, mapping, reflecting, magnifying, even prying—that ensures anyone who wants to explore what it means to live boldly can find a way to do so."
—Ellen Notbohm, author of *Ten Things Every Child with Autism Wishes You Knew*

"*Live Boldly* comes to us at a time it is needed most. Indeed, it calls upon us to bring out our best and provides the tools to do so. Mary Anne's stories, written with such grace and power, made me laugh, touched my heart—even gave me goosebumps. What more could you ask of a book?"
—Tony Burroughs, author of *The Code: 10 Intentions for a Better World*

"Like a Christmas tree sparkling with colored lights, *Live Boldly* offers countless words, phrases, quotations, and stories to further anyone's psycho-spiritual growth, however far they may be along their path."
—Frank Andrews, author of *The Art and Practice of Loving*

live Boldly

cultivate the qualities that can change your life

mary anne radmacher

Conari Press

First published in 2008 by Conari Press,
an imprint of Red Wheel/Weiser, LLC

With offices at:
500 Third Street, Suite 230
San Francisco, CA 94107
www.redwheelweiser.com

ISBN: 978-1-57324-321-6

LIBRARY OF CONGRESS CATALOGING-IN-PUBLICATION DATA
Available upon request

Cover and text design by Maxine Ressler
Typeset in Adobe Garamond
Cover illustration and hand lettering © Mary Anne Radmacher

Printed in Canada
FR
10 9 8 7 6 5 4 3 2 1

To Susan Pfeiffer of Little Rock, Arkansas,
who acted upon her vision with clarity
blesses me with a legacy of friendship.
Susan "sent me in" during her final seconds
in the game.

To Connie Fails, who had the boldness to
accept the transfer of position.
The whole lot of Singers who
let me hum along.

contents

introduction
living as if no one is looking

Your fundamental character may be what you do when you *think* no one is watching. Thomas Jefferson asserted that truth. To live boldly is to create a synthesis between your observed and unobserved life.

I asked everybody in my symbol class to think of themselves dancing. To imagine how they move and what their patterns are in those movements. Then I asked them to draw a line showing that pattern of movement. And a hand raised. Question?

"Do you want us to draw our dancing when people are watching us or when we are dancing alone?"

I'll thank him again for asking that question. Dance is a mighty fine metaphor for living boldly. *Live Boldly* is an admonition to allow your desires and illuminating natural character to overshadow your sense of being watched, of standing in the judgment of others. That awareness of scrutiny is less about reputation than it is a fundamental desire for approval. If self-validation were our most significant measure, we would give trophies to ourselves, not watch celebrities receive them on TV. I wouldn't have to ask prominent and recognizable people to endorse my books. *I wrote it. . . . I* will endorse it for you. I would recommend it by virtue of having taken the time to create it and offer it to you.

"But what will the neighbors think?" is a question that many people ask, almost unconsciously. Many decisions are based upon this inquiry and the concern it represents: "What will people say?" The strength of public opinion can be important, but the key in living boldly is being able to discern when it doesn't matter a tweak. I love the way Dr. Seuss said it: "Be who you are and say what you feel because those who mind don't matter and those who matter don't mind."

Said another way, living boldly is living as if no one were watching you. And then . . . not having your actions change when you know people *are* watching.

Live Boldly.

I was asked, earnestly, by a mother of two who had just married again, "*How is it* you have what it takes to live so boldly, and other people seem so timid? What *is* that?"

I answered, "I have a tremendous capacity for failure." She gasped. It wasn't anything she expected to hear. I continued, "Which is to say, I see failure as an opportunity to learn. To try something different. And I have the capacity to see failure as an element in the process of my own growth. I learn from it. I move on. I see the failure, but I do not identify myself as a failure."

The questioner objected. "But how—how can you move into a new thing fully knowing you might fail?"

"Because I move into a new thing knowing I might succeed. But I'm willing, *willing* to fail."

The most insidious failures I have experienced are the ones in which I never risked the trying. Then I was left to live with the wondering of what might have been. Winston Churchill lived by what he is known for saying: "Success is the ability to go from failure to failure without losing your enthusiasm." Indeed.

A health plan trying to promote physical activity created a billboard campaign announcing that the real victory occurs when you cross the starting line. I say it differently: "Hitting the ball out of the park and having the courage to pick up the bat-they're the same thing. Go ahead—pick up the bat."

To live boldly encompasses many things. An invitation to act true to your nature, to act in accord with your natural strengths. Absent that, it is the vision to begin to act in accord with your inclination, seeking out that thing you would like to *be*, or *face*, even when the natural ability, or the courage, isn't yet within your grasp. Living boldly is walking right into the thing you need at the moment . . . and putting it on. Seeing how well you can make it fit.

Jan, one of my long-time friends, shared her opinion of boldly taking on a quality you don't naturally possess. Laughing, she said, "Well, you know, Mary Anne, there are some things in life that I actually can control and change. And the rest of the stuff I just run away from." She was only being half-silly. We all run from something. Living boldly is about stopping yourself in the midst of your run.

Stop.

Think about what you are running from.

Turn around.

Look at it. Reach for your personal tool kit.

Take it on.

Taking something on with boldness might even mean running! Who knows? Only you know the right tool . . . and I sincerely hope my words work together with your good thinking and produce results you are pleased with.

Living Boldly doesn't mean living LOUDLY. As in my aphorism:

> courage doesn't always roar.
> sometimes courage is the quiet voice at the
> end of the day saying,
> "i will try again tomorrow."

so it is to live boldly. The impact is somewhat counterintuitive. People tell me they think of living boldly as living loud(ly). Not so. Think of the breath a wind instrument player uses—it must be full. *Bold.* That doesn't mean it produces a loud sound. It means it produces a full sound, as the musician intended. Of course, loud is always an option.

An assertive, rough-around-the-edges client sat before me. Disciplined and accomplished as a yoga practitioner, she expressed frustration that she was so *loud.* That she was not calmer, quieter, gentler. It was a simple thing for me to remind her that the calm and quiet people often have the same longing for the trumpet and trombone of her parade. I celebrated her strengths and asked her to find ways to take those very qualities and make them work more effectively for her. Work with them instead of against them.

School systems often require students to attempt to master the very thing in which they perform most poorly. What would happen to our students if we provided them with the most intense instruction in the subject at which they excel? If we took their "better" and made it the "best"? What would happen to you if you did that for yourself?

Living boldly is an exercise, a practice in reaching for qualities that will help you strengthen what is already strong within you but may need a little muscle work, some fine-tuning. It's also a way to identify what is not naturally present in you (or only present in what seems small measure) and put it there. Borrow it, in a sense, if only for a day.

To live boldly suggests that you can outfit your soul for the journey of your dreams or for the unusual demands of a particular day. That you can identify the qualities and characteristics that you need *today*, to live closer to the

dream,
   to accomplish the thing that scares you,
      to act in accord with your true and illuminated self.

In other words, to dance more closely to the way you *really* dance, when you think no one is looking. And here, perhaps, is a most important awareness: There is someone who is almost always looking—and it is you.

Ah, dance as if no one is looking. Jan and I were speaking of her nineteen-year-old daughter. For perspective, we remembered some of our shared experiences when we were nineteen. "Boy, remember that one time when you led the whole congregation in a dance?" she said. "And then you just danced by yourself? Remember that? That was so brave." She was serious. She meant *brave*. For me, it was a matter of answering the longing of my heart. To express in movement what was hard for my young soul to find words to express. I had no training. No guidance. No choreography skills at all. Not even, really, a lot of grace. Certainly not the body of a dancer. Just the willingness to act boldly, as if no one were looking. Jan called it "being brave." And over thirty years later, she still remembers that day.

Think of those times when you see something that really moves you, and you say to yourself, "Wow, I wish I had the nerve to do that!" That's an invitation to your own boldness. An invitation for *you* to discover what it would take for you to be able to do the thing *you* long for. I'm just sharing some of my starting points—only you know what it will take for you.

Live boldly before yourself so you live through your day to that just-before-sleep moment where you offer yourself the certain approval, "Today I have done my best." That's when you get to present yourself a trophy. A trophy for living boldly forward in your day—living as if no one were looking.

how to use this book

In the following chapters, I present reflections on things that require boldness for me. Please look at them through the windows of your own experiences. You can read them straight through, or open them wherever you feel inclined. At the end of each reflection, I will pull a suggestion or two out of my "tool kit." I offer these to you as a way to implement the desire to live boldly, to make it more practical. In the afterword, there are additional ideas on how to personalize this process. The types of suggestions are outlined below, and each has its own symbol.

Magnifying glass: A series of questions that make the thing you are boldly living into . . . bigger, clearer, more defined.

Segue/Small map: A suggestion of something to do to take you from one place to another. I know the word "segue" through stand-up comedy. The term refers to a way to get from one segment of content to another. It's an Italian word that means a short path. That path is represented here by a small map.

Mirror: Reflection, suggestions of things to think on. Also, one often looks externally for reasons or understanding. The mirror symbol suggests the answer lies within you.

Pen: Many people have said that they write to find out what they think. So often, students share with me the discovery that they didn't know a certain thing was true for them or about them . . . until they started writing about it. This tool can be used in so many ways. Here I will provide suggestions of ways to write toward bold living.

Icon: A physical object or universal sign/symbol that helps you focus on your intention toward boldness. I often carry a heart-shaped rock that my husband gave me, as a reminder that I am surrounded by love. This symbol ⊘ is universally understood to mean *no*.

Trophy: A way to reward yourself or someone else. Living boldly may achieve recognition from others, but it recognizes that the most important validation comes from within. It is also a reminder of the key role expressing gratitude and appreciation plays.

Crowbar: Anybody who has ever used one knows it's an excellent tool to pry something open. Use this tool category to pry yourself loose from your habit(s), assumptions, and conventional ways.

Open book: A poetic reflection pertaining to a particular desired quality. Write one of your own . . . or focus on the one in the book. Carry it with you in the course of your day and see what insight it might open for you.

make the reflections yours

In safety, without harshness or unfair judgments, by yourself, take the opportunity to look at *your* need (identify). It helps to define it. Understand how others see it. (Check out a biography of an individual who articulates or demonstrates this particular quality. Learn what someone you admire said about it.) Define it for yourself. (Ask, "What does it mean to me?") Express your understanding of it in context (say it in a sentence), or express it poetically (say it beautifully). Think of a time when this strength has been used in a life experience (tell a story about it). Ask questions about it (make inquiry).

Ask yourself what you would look like and how you would act if you were demonstrating that skill . . . and then create ways to step boldly into that circumstance with the strengths/ skills you have borrowed. Or accessed. Or recognized. I call it borrowing because sometimes I am not aware that I already hold that particular quality within my being. Frequently, in the course of this process, I discover elements of that particular thing within me . . . abilities I didn't previously recognize were there.

These exercises make a great beginning. Go ahead. Cultivate the qualities that can change your life.

Live boldly.
laugh loudly.
love truly.
play as often as you can.
work as smart as you are able.
share your heart as deeply
as you can reach.
choose in ways that support
your dreams.
honor your actions (perceived
as success or failure)
as your teachers.

as you awaken may your
dreams greet you by name
and may you answer,
"yes!"

as you walk may angels gather
at your shoulders
and may you know
they stand with you.
as you rest.
may all your endeavors be
rooted in contentment and peace.

live boldly

mission

noun. an important assignment carried out for political, religious, or commercial purposes.

He who has a why to live for can bear almost any how.
—Friedrich Nietzsche

---

dare to dream of your great success. become intimate with those things which deeply motivate you and regularly work toward the realization of that mission.

—mary anne radmacher (mar)

In the overwhelming press of possibility and projects, there comes a question.

"What is the single illuminating thing which shines its light on all the elements of the best parts of your life (the sound of which makes your heart sing and your feet dance)?" Answer that and then know: that is the thing you must do.

When I think of a person's mission, I think in terms of a corporate motto or mission statement. As a metaphor, it works to think of myself as a corporate entity. I have lots of departments within my being that all carry out different tasks. The banner above all that work is the single purpose of the corporation, the measure by which work is accepted or rejected. If you don't like the corporate analogy, you can look at the mission on a personal level and call it "the one illuminating thing." When I am connected to that thing, it is very clear. My commitment and ease in any activity is immediate and visible.

One should not confuse their mission with goal setting. Goals emerge as a result of understanding what your mission is . . . what fundamentally inspires virtually all the actions and activities of your life? I know what mine is—what is yours? While the sense of mission can have a religious tone, it is not solely limited to that. My mission is to inspire and be inspired. Inspiration is the word of my mission. That touches on the realm of spirit, but it is not only there that it lives. On my best days, inspiration expresses itself through all my choices.

I had the opportunity to be interviewed by Timberly Whitfield on her show, *New Morning*. There was a flurry of advance preparation—many telephone calls with her producer and lots of information exchanged. Television production is very tied to specific timing and deadline. Yet, as I spoke with my contact, Caroline, I was impressed by her profound attentiveness and calm. Her level of calm was so amazing that I finally asked her to identify her process. I wanted to feature it in a section about focus. As I watched her identify and unfold her process, I saw that what Caroline was really defining was her mission, her fundamental illuminating thing that makes so many other qualities shine. She also thought at first that she was talking about prioritizing and focus. Of course, she addressed attentiveness and lists and keeping the important things straight in her head, but upon deeper and continued reflection, she shared this with me:

I started to think more deeply about the ideas of focus and prioritizing in connection to my core relationship with God, and I realized that there is an outward manifestation of my faith in my day-to-day work life that I'm not completely aware of. But I believe this is what it is: every person I encounter is a reflection of the divine. And therefore, not only is there an instantaneous and deep level of respect for that person, but there is also a "kindredness," a recognition that occurs.

So that's the foundation from which the peace (and apparent focus) springs. Then there is a discerning, again—not necessarily conscious, but still very real—"What does this person need? How can I make him/her feel comfortable so we can work well together?" When people are brought into a unique situation, one which they've never been in before (being on TV, for example), they are looking for direction, for encouragement and for compassion. I reach to give that to that person, each and every time. It is not always easy, figuring out what a person needs, and you have to do that in a split second in TV land. It can occur in an instant over the phone, by the person's voice or choice of language. But I draw often on my previous experience when I was a music manager. In that capacity I learned how to pull a note out of a symphony, a lyric or word out of a composition, a rhythmic sequence from an entire bass line, listening to music and learning from a music producer. I also had to learn to read him pretty well, too. I learned to use laser beam technique similar to the one he used in music to establish a better communication between us and ultimately between myself and everyone with whom I work. I am extremely grateful for that experience—learning to produce from a master producer.

Those are the spiritual and psychological components for me.

Meanwhile, there are the deadlines and the rush-rush-rush demands of production that must be met in order for me and everyone else to get the job done. So this is where the prioritizing comes in: what needs to happen right now? And then what will happen next? And who needs what before when? Part of this thought process comes from doing this for a while—there is a certain rhythm, a certain "punch list" that you need to hit for each and every story. I make a template for every show I work on so that it includes all the basic necessities, from making sure the elements are legally sound to transportation needs for each guest. It always helps to write it down. Write out everything you need or think you might need. You need to anticipate a different scenario and know how you'll respond. A good example: What if my guest is delayed by weather or suddenly can't make the show? Who's my back-up? How do I follow up with the travel arrangements I made and don't want to be socked for? What changes do I need to make in the script right now?

As a producer, you need to be prepared with a Plan B. And if you're doing live TV, plan on Plans C-Z, too. That comes with experience and the unadulterated understanding that things will *happen* and things will *change* at the last minute, and that's just the nature of the beast. You can't fight it. You have to be willing to let the chips fall where they may and trust, implicitly, that it will work regardless.

That's where the faith comes back in—can't shake it. Because who am I to say I will control this situation? Who am I to say that I can control anything in life, including my own? You have to roll with it. And there's that ease again, that peace again. Because even if I fail, and I will, oh boy, will I! That still, small voice says, "I am with you, I will never abandon you or forsake you. It's going to be fine." And it's that realization that takes me even deeper: my *identity* cannot be shaken by circumstances or opinions or natural disasters or bad TV. My core is a harbor for the Peace I have been left.

A friend was talking about sanctification the other day. The down and dirty work that you and the Spirit have to do together to refine your soul. And, in a way, that's exactly what my work is about. Heck, it's what life is about! It's painful, exciting, scary, and ultimately glorious. That reflection of the divine will simply get clearer and more vivid the more you're doing the work and trusting that the God of the Universe has your back, and therefore, oh yes, therefore, everything really is just fine, fine, fine.

—Caroline Sprinkel Santangelo

• tool kit •

Listen to the stories you tell repeatedly. What do they tell you about yourself? Do they relate to your mission? What are your most amazing accomplishments so far? What accomplishments give you the most satisfaction? Do they relate to your mission?

If you had a motto, what would it be? Remember, a company's motto is the thing by which they choose and measure their actions.

Perspective

noun. 1. the art of drawing solid objects on a two-dimensional surface so as to give the right impression of their height, width, depth, and position in relation to each other. 2. a particular attitude toward or way of regarding something; a point of view.

A rock pile ceases to be a rock pile the moment a single man contemplates it, bearing within him the image of a cathedral.

—Antoine de Saint-Exupéry

live as if this is all there is.

—mar

How may I spend this day that it may have consequence beyond my own embrace?

People say it all the time. No matter how bad things are, there's always somebody who's got it worse than you. And I ask myself, "Is that supposed to make me feel better?" Well, yes. It is. And it should. But—it doesn't always.

Perspective, which is a particular attitude toward something, is the greater thing to which many aspire. Seeing a singular or small element in the context of a larger vision or mission is perspective. While the element may be a disappointment in itself, set within the "bigger picture" or "the larger perspective," it becomes part of the process.

Who do you know that always seems to be in cadence with their own plans? When surprises come along, they are able to incorporate them into the rhythm and just keep on. Perspective. There's a reason that coaches talk about this in their team vocabulary a lot. It's an essential component for winning. Players have to bring a certain point of view to the game, and this is true in any sort of setting. Your point of view sets you up well in advance for how you view the events as they unfold.

It's an old phrase, familiar and true: Things are either stumbling blocks or stepping stones. Unexpected events can set you back or set you up. It's all a matter of—perspective.

Anyone who's benefited from a Twelve Step program recognizes the assessment, "It's your best thinking that got you here." Einstein asserted that it's a sure sign of insanity if you think the same actions are going to produce different results.

Perspective sometimes requires dramatic assistance. And the courage to step outside of your own immediate comfort or habits of thinking.

• tool kit •

I've used a writing exercise for years to expand my perspective and stretch my point of view beyond my natural borders. I call this exercise "The Board of Directors." Recently a student pointed out he'd be more comfortable using the metaphor of a construction site and the various roles there. Whatever works. Take the intent of the exercise and put it in the context of your own experience.

I utilize people whose views are admired by me but different from mine. And I ask them, in theory, to "serve" on my board. The board of my life's perspective. In theory, I say, because not all of them are living. In fact, some of them are imaginary. But I sure can use their perspectives. When I come to a wall or block in my experience or thinking . . . I reach out to someone on my board. Emerson, Eleanor Roosevelt, Anne Morrow Lindbergh, Bill Clinton, and Mark Twain are some of the folks who consistently serve on my board.

I've used the practice so much I no longer need to go through the process of writing. It just comes to mind.

I ask myself, "What would Eleanor advise me to do in this situation?" My perspective is instantly transported outside my own parameters.

Who serves on your board? When you identify them, start putting them to work right away.

When my friends Suze and Jonathan got married, I gave them an unusual gift—a pair of opera glasses outfitted with prisms instead of long-distance lenses. I told them to use these glasses when they were having a disagreement. Why? Because a prism provides so many different images of a single view. It is a literal reminder that while *one* thing may be the subject of the argument, there can be so many different ways of looking at it. Use the icon of the prism to bring perspective to any issue that requires you to live boldly. Perhaps you can make a list of at least a dozen different ways the same thing could be "seen" or considered.

Vision

noun. 1. the faculty or state of being able to see. 2. the ability to think about or plan the future with imagination or wisdom. 3. a mental image of what the future will or could be like.

If a man hasn't discovered something that he will die for, he isn't fit to live.

—Martin Luther King Jr.

---

vision: to expect a greater standard, a better result; to step up, peer over the shoulders of what is ordinary and get a good sighting on what is possible. to act with vision is to dare and believe a greater thing will unfold before you as you clear your sight.

—mar

At twenty-seven I was still convinced that I'd have to wait until I was at least forty to have enough money and accumulated knowledge to start my own company. My father always said I should either start my own greeting card company or else buy stock in one. From as young an age as eight, I would purchase my own cards at the neighborhood drugstore and rewrite the text on the inside. Go figure. Skill sets come out early, don't they?

At twenty-eight years of age, with fifteen dollars as the total of my holdings, I began my company with eighteen images and a great deal of vision. The accumulated education would present itself over the coming decades. It was a stroke of fortune that I didn't know anything about business when I started my company. If I had grasped cash flows and initial investments and market trends, I'm certain I would have "known better" and never have begun.

After a few years in business, I made the significant investment and started showing my work at the industry's pinnacle trade show: the New York stationery show. I met a woman named Susan Pfeiffer. What a character. How much she knew about art and an artist's heart. The first time she walked up to me, it was as if I were being greeted by an old friend. Over time, that's what Susan became.

Before I tell you the rest of the story let me tell you this . . .

When President Clinton was elected the first time, I created a card in his honor. It read, "Change, of any sort, requires courage. I remember a place called HOPE." I told the members of my staff that someday I would be creating my work especially for President Clinton. No one scoffed, but it seemed fairly out of reach. My friend, Dr. Deanna Davis, would say that I was taking "inspired action," an important element in using the Law of Attraction.

Susan and I shared a mutual friend who I would not meet for years to come. Connie Fails. These two woman shared knowledge of my product and my work. When the time came to build a presidential library, and the Clintons asked Connie to step forward and create their museum store, Connie said yes.

Susan offered her help and both women decided, out of all the lettering artists in the country, to call me and ask if I would select and render some of President Clinton's quotes for the store. Over the years, many people had asked me to do this very thing. The answer was always no. Thank you, but no. My business vision tied my unique signature lettering style to my own original writings and no one else's words. Very clear-cut. And it made saying "no!" easy for years.

Then, Connie called. My strategically prepared answer and way of thinking about my business changed instantly.

I am not a political junkie. But when an issue moves me, or a candidate who stands for my values stands up . . . I put my shoulders behind their vision. William Jefferson Clinton was such a stand-up candidate. In the early nineties, anybody who knew me knew that, given less than ninety seconds, I was going to tell them about this governor from Arkansas that the United States needed as their leader. And we got him.

In the very instant for which I had trained myself to say *no*, I said *yes*. Yes. I would be honored to be the scribe of President Clinton's words. I would be thrilled to place his timeless observations into a format which would bring his words into the homes and offices and classrooms of thousands of people. This man is artful in his communication, and I would bring my best artfulness to this project. And I did. I had my own collection of Clinton quotes all ready to go. His words had long inspired me. Both as a writer and as a citizen.

That could have been the end of this story. But it's not. Actually it's where this story of vision begins.

Ten days before the opening of the Clinton Library in Little Rock, Susan Pfeiffer called me and, in her summery way, said, "Hey by the way, I'm dying with a bazillion different things and I'm not sure which one is going to get me first. But I've had a vision and I know that I'm supposed to bring you to Little Rock and send you to the Library opening, and I need to give you, as a gift, to my dearest friend, Connie Fails; this is really important and I know you're busy and this is short notice but . . . won't you come?" Her sentence may have been a little longer than that! Just as she packed a lot into a life, she packed many ideas into a few sentences.

Of course I went. I was supposed to be "gifted" to Connie, but in truth, she was gifted to me. Connie was Susan Pfeiffer's dying gift to me. Connie got a cool necklace from Susan, and I got Connie. I was gifted with the friendship of Paul and Linda Leopoulos. And over time, many of the fine souls affiliated with this work have come to my shoulder and I am honored to know them.

I came and I worked at the Presidential Museum store. I stocked. I inventoried. I took my decades of retail experience and was welcomed into the nascent team at the store who did not grasp that thousands of people were going to line up around the block and come to purchase a little piece of an extraordinary history. There weren't enough hands to keep the shelves stocked with all the pieces of the life of President Clinton that these folks wanted to carry away. In between stocking, I pulled my pencil out and signed the posters. And personalized them. It was a magical time.

Through a series of remarkable turns of events . . . I was at the Clinton Library during its opening ceremony. I was one of the few people who were warm and dry. I stood ten feet from Bono singing. I wept as he sang "Sunday, Bloody Sunday." (That man expresses his vision beautifully through his music.) I was moved, then, by all that this past president was accomplishing in the world, and I couldn't really have begun to imagine how far his reach would continue to go through his foundation work. But that day, standing seventy-five feet away from the podium containing a historic collection of presidents, I would have believed that anything was possible. After all, look where I was standing—speaking of anything being possible. Eleven days earlier, my plans were completely different. Susan called. There was vision. Things changed.

Turns out, with President Clinton anything is possible. Why not gather together the most powerful people in the world and make them pay to make the world a better place, ask them to make a commitment to change and then hold them accountable to their promise on a global stage? Why not call that a Global Initiative and rock the world with it? Why not? Why not have the vision and then put the courage behind it to make it come to fruition? And as for vision—it came right back to my personal experience in that building, that day. I was there because Susan had the vision of it, and the guts to act upon what she saw. Turns out Susan Pfeiffer believed anything is possible, too.

Later, I spent hours poring over small typeface in large leather-bound volumes of President Clinton's public words, looking for those phrases which stay with people's hearts and inspire them every day. One of my favorites buried in some insignificant speech from the early nineties: "Nothing big ever came from being small."

In that Choctaw Building, I got to see the history, the diversity, the incredible breadth of personality, skill, motivation, and talent of those who are drawn to the side of President Clinton. While working in that building, I thought several times of my friend Susan, and her vision for me in Little Rock. I shook my head. That woman had the guts to put her shoulders behind her vision and push. And now I was studying the words of a man who does the same thing globally. In that building, I got to see for myself, up close, why the greatness of people with vision isn't a myth but practical reality.

And in that building, I got to meet President Clinton.

After I met him, briefly chatted, and didn't drop over from . . . whatever happens when you encounter a great mind and global presence such as his . . . after that, I got to watch why I believed in him in 1991 and why I still believe in him. He was prompted to leave by the big guy behind him with a big watch. It took three points to the watch to get President Clinton to leave me and the whole Choctaw staff . . . but he ambled down the stairs. And stopped to speak with *every single* guest in the foyer. Those guests who came because they wanted to see the building. Who had no idea that they were going to meet one of the finest presidents America will ever see. All those folks, in their excitement, pressed and crowded in front of a small, disabled gentleman, who was pushed to the corner, unseen. I could see because I was leaning over the mezzanine. But on the floor, President Clinton was simply flanked by adoring guests.

He doesn't need a mezzanine view to see humanity. Nope. He really doesn't. I saw him work through the crowd, heading not for the door (to the dismay of the large man with the watch) but to the corner. To the physically challenged man. With his back to the press of the crowd, President Clinton gave the bulk of his time (of which he had none to spare, as the large man would have told you) to this gentleman, who would have been overlooked by most others.

I was crying. Again. And I looked at Stephanie, the executive director of the Clinton Foundation. She smiled and said that now I would have a better understanding of what is meant by running on Clinton time. She said that, at the end of the day, what we were watching happen right then was what made her work so hard at her job.

Everybody picks things to believe in. I believe I'll believe in this. That the most powerful find it the easiest to reach to the most small. And that is just one of the secrets of William Jefferson Clinton's great strength and profound vision. And I'll believe that anyone who is willing to put the press of action behind their vision can achieve amazing things. Anyone. Susan Pfeiffer. President Clinton. Me. You.

Just days after these events, Susan Pfeiffer succumbed to one of her "bazillion" ailments.

Years later, the foundation offered my teaching skills as a contribution to the Arkansas Literary Festival. On April 21, 2007, I was honored that Susan's gift to me, my kindredness with Connie Fails, made it possible to have the national release of my first book in Little Rock, Arkansas. After a book signing in the museum store, we celebrated in the very foyer where I saw President Clinton reach out to the gentleman in the corner.

I had a quiet place reserved for a woman who believed in and acted upon her vision. A woman who knew the power of acting on a dream, and whose action helped me realize my vision of many years earlier. I do indeed create work on behalf of William Jefferson Clinton. An unlikelihood, a thing made of seemingly wishful thinking, became my experience. And one of the finest stories in my life.

first
you must
    learn to see
        unseeing;
once you move blind
    you learn to
        move with
            sight.

laugh loudly

gratitude

noun. the quality of being thankful; readiness to show appreciation for and to return kindness; gratefulness, thankfulness, thanks, appreciation, indebtedness; recognition, acknowledgment, credit.

As we express our gratitude, we must never forget that the highest appreciation is not to utter words, but to live by them.

—John Fitzgerald Kennedy

---

yes. as the evening beckons with the promise of tomorrow . . . may your gratitude rise up and with strength answer,
*   "yes."*

—mar

This day boldness is manifested in a simple grace:
gratitude.
While lost in my awareness of all I do not have in this
moment . . .
I walked past a man who barely had use of his legs . . .
and perhaps not all of his good brain. . . .
and suddenly the wealth of what I do have overcame me.

Today I offer a prayer of forgiveness:
forgive the pettiness of my ingratitude . . .
the absence of profound thankfulness.
A wise child understands the real nature of plenty and does
not
foolishly ask for MORE.

How the process of making May Day baskets in my childhood became associated with expressing gratitude I cannot be certain. It just did. Perhaps it was a seed a well-intended person planted in my thinking. Or maybe it was just my way of making sense out of building paper baskets, picking flowers, and hanging them, anonymously, on people's doorknobs.

For the longest time, I thought gratitude was something that had to be extended to another for it to be legitimate. Just like the literal act of hanging a flower basket on a door knob. The power of gratitude has grown in my life. I appreciate its boldness in the quiet, unspoken depths and its ability to buoy another by being articulated.

Gratitude wears many guises in my life experience. One of its most powerful applications is to experience gratitude for difficulties and hardship. The turning point often comes when I stop resisting and embrace the challenge, grateful for the ways it is teaching me. Gratitude can change everything.

Gratitude is also acknowledgment. How many times have you said to yourself, after the fact, "I wish I would have told that person at the service station how grateful I was for her cleaning my windshield?" Such a little thing. A small gesture. What keeps you from speaking a gratitude such as that? Acknowledgment is water on a garden. It can make a big difference.

Gratitude can mean returning a kindness. Expressing gratitude seems like a cosmic invitation for all kinds of thankfulness and appreciation to pour in. Opening a door, just a crack, lets a great deal of light into a darkened room.

Voltaire said, "Appreciation is a wonderful thing. It makes what is excellent in others belong to us, as well."

• tool kit •

How can it change an experience to look for gratitudes? What are the things that you are most
grateful for in your life? Who are the people in your life
that draw out your gratitude? Is there a difference in
your experience when you quietly reflect on your gratitudes and when you decide to express them out loud or
in action?

Once a week, write out some of your gratitudes. Or in the spirit of living boldly, write
out the things you *want* to experience gratitude toward.
Post them in visible places: dashboard, mirror, planner
book, wallet. Reflect on them often. Notice if there is a
shift in your thinking.

Send a note of gratitude to someone you have
never met.

Release

verb. 1. allow or enable to escape from confinement; set free. 2. remove restrictions or obligations from (someone or something). 3. allow (something) to return to its resting position by ceasing to put pressure on it. 4. surrender.

He is no fool who gives up what he cannot keep to gain what he cannot lose.

—Jim Eliott

---

persevere. plan. strategize. focus. breathe. write. let go: relax. forgive. all this failing: take a nap.

—mar

The waitress looks out the window disapprovingly. Hands on her hips, she assesses, "The fog did lift a little. But now it's just—" she breaks off.

I finish, "hovering?"

Emphatically, she corrects me: "Covering."

"Ah."

"Every day I hope for sun, and this—" she gestures to the space over the sea, which seems to be magically or mechanically in high production of rolling fog, "this is what I get!"

"Isn't this how Point Lobos always is?" I ask.

"Well, yes," she reluctantly agrees. "But I keep hoping. I've been here since" (*wait for it!*) "1959 and I just can't get used to the fog."

I'm barely able to keep my roar of laughter in check. I've just been reading of the stoics' "logos," the spirit of accepting "what is." And I've been thinking on the Tao "moving in the way of the way things are." After all that, this is just too ironic. Still, I manage to offer, feebly, "Maybe tomorrow."

"Yes. Tomorrow. Perhaps tomorrow," she murmurs as she skirts away to the next hungry customer. How many more years would she hold on tightly to her hope that Point Lobos would be without fog?

In one day I let go decades of held expectations as to what it meant to live a "writer's life." I kept waiting for a calmer, more purposeful way of writing. A quieter life. A life that matched the reflective quality of my poetry. I kept waiting. Did I mention waiting? I waited a long time. And then, one day of no apparent consequence, while speaking about this to my friend Jonathan, I heard something in my own conversation so monumental that it allowed me to release all those silly expectations. I heard the truth in my own simple words: "What if this life *is* my writing life?"

That day I wrote: Yes. Perhaps today I have decided to be a writer.

You find that odd, since my writings have been circulating for decades and are in tens of thousands of homes and offices and school rooms? Well, let me tell you what I mean.

I can no longer wait to "live a writing life." This life is my writing life. I own a small business. I have professional associates. I have dogs that don't much care how close I am to capturing an elusive thought in just the right phrase. If they have to pee, they have to pee. That's just the way it is.

I have idealized the writing life for almost as long as I have been writing. When I wrote "it's raining" in second grade, perhaps I did not hold a fully formed expectation of what it would be like to devote the whole of my energies to writing—but maybe when I wrote the interactive courtroom drama in fourth grade, I was starting to form a picture. Early on, I confused writing and art, and, as it happens, I have been confused ever since. Mostly I think I am a writer, but then there are all those framed pieces with my name on them, which would indicate I am an artist.

Today, I understand that everything I do, every day, is my writing life. Living a writing life isn't about a sanctuary, decorated beautifully, with things catalogued in order. My journals and writings are spread, willy-nilly, in my garage, in boxes in the back room, in files with mystifying names—names that made sense to me when I wrote them, names that seemed so important I thought I would remember them in minute detail. And now, when I happen upon them while looking for my tax record (which also seems to be filed in a willy-nilly fashion), I can't begin to explain to myself what I might have been thinking.

What I have come to understand this particular day is that I have really been dreaming of being rested, not of writing for ten hours a day, every day, for the rest of my life. And I understand this now because I have recently gifted myself with the opportunity of rest. Of respite. Of withdrawing from the hyper press and production of, well, my production company. (Maybe I should start calling it a writing life company instead of a production company, just to reinforce this fresh view.)

The insight that knocked on my door today—and fortunately I was at home, resting, so I could answer the door—was this: I have to live the stuff to write about it. This is not a mapping headquarters, set upon a high hill, from which I never venture out. This is guerilla play. This is harsh business. This is compassionate exchange and gang members and homeless people approaching me on the street. This is a crazy man driving past me on an early Saturday morning and driving into the foyer of the courthouse kitty-corner from my business.

Life is full of craziness, of cars driving places they don't belong, of rifles at the ready. Life is full of the stuff that makes writers write. Should I be concerned about that? I'd say yes. It's all my concern—to see it, live it, rub around in it like the grass upon which my Labrador rolls and rubs, mingling his scent with the scent of the grass. That kind of concern, the kind that gets grass stains on my pants. And then, later, I'll write about it.

That's a writing life, or, at the very best, it is *my* writing life. And in knowing this, I am able to release all those other ideas about a different sort of life, a life I have to wait for. This way, there's no waiting. It's here. Boldly, I get to step into it and walk with it.

• tool kit •

Look at and listen to yourself. Pay attention to the kinds of questions you ask about your life when you are talking to your friends. Sometimes the things you really want sneak in the back door. Notice.

Wonder what opportunities you pass, unwittingly, because your hands are so busy clasping what you think you have always known. Unwilling to let go, to release this small certainty you hold . . . you miss the chance to hold treasures.

Release the thing you must . . . in a physical and representative way. Write on a small piece of paper that thing you carry which you wish you did not. Build a small fire (in an appropriate environment, please) and burn that thing. Sometimes the physical act leads to the shift in view.

This experience can be emulated, digitally, on a Web site I really enjoy.

http://www.myinnerworld.com. There, Michelle Bernhardt (author of *Colorstrology*) offers you the digital opportunity to write out your worries and woes and release them to the fire. Both experiences can accomplish the same thing.

love truly

noun. 1. an intense feeling of deep affection. 2. a deep
attachment to someone.

I want to love first, and live incidentally.

—Zelda Fitzgerald

---

*go ahead. weep for the rare, the never seen this way
again, the excruciating, ineffable, unmitigated beauty
of love.*

—mar

I glance up from the work table in my living room. This table which balances books and journals and love letters and correspondence and music and creating with pens and brushes and colors.

Dusk falls. The room grows dark. I have been in the chair, gluing squares, and thinking about my words and my world. Realizing that off and on for twenty years I've been gluing these little squares on my writings, painting them and sending them out to the world.

And this day I see that pretty much all my correspondences are love letters. That loving is the most unmitigatedly courageous act I perform in a day. Looking at the peach and champagne amber colors of sunset peering through the old tree branches outside my window . . . I contemplate the beauty of the reflection which I enjoy in a mirror on the wall. The metaphor is rich, for that reflection is of both my husband and me.

Many of my closest friends realize that they should send a thank-you note to my Labrador retriever, Judah. That dog was my coach on love and loving. And a fine coach, indeed. From the day that Judah ran across a field and jumped into my arms, wondering what took me so long to come for him . . . to the day that he leapt into my arms after going to live with some of my best friends in Illinois (again asking me what took me so long to come see him), that four-legged trainer has given me daily lessons on the value of consistent demonstrations of my love.

What keeps those words from leaping easily to our lips—those unreserved, elaborate broad expressions of our love and esteem? I used to justify my reticence to say, "I love you," as a matter of the words being unnecessary. They know I love them, I would reason.

Some knowledge bears repeating. Reinforcing. I advocate speaking words of love with all the sincerity that can be mustered, as frequently as possible. And my soulmate, my dear husband, continues Judah's work in helping me speak what my heart knows to be true. Not on an anniversary. Not for a special occasion. Just because it's true, I say as often as I can in as many different ways as I can form, "I sure love you."

Or, try this. *Slow down.* Gift the love of your life with your undistracted, untelevisioned, unhurried attentiveness. If you plan on saying "I love you," then pause, yes, slow down, and look at that person whom you call your love, and at a focused pace . . . say the words. Don't rush off to some other "next" thing. Pause. Lovingness shouldn't "fit in" to your life . . . your lifeness, even for a little while, should fit around your love. Try in the spirit of nurturing.

Ask yourself to slow down.
Pay a little more attention. Notice how increased attentiveness impacts your experience.

Speak the words you deeply know . . . but don't often say.

Wrap up a small box and set it out to remind yourself. Create more than one special surprise. And let some of the surprises come early. (A valentine *on* Valentine's day isn't *exactly* a surprise, if you know what I mean.) Surprise yourself with all the ways you can think of today to boldly demonstrate love to the important relationships in your life.

Friendship

noun. 1. the emotions or behavior of friends.
2. relationship. association. bond. tie.

Raise the bridge, my friend is sailing by.
—Rod McKuen

---

a holiday, the day i first named you, "friend."
—mar

Here's a confession. I draw upon a wealth of material by listening (unobtrusively) to conversations in coffee shops. There, more than any other place, I hear people discussing broken friendships. Even more than chatter about dating or love lives . . . friendship takes the top berth in the conversation train.

"I thought we were friends."

"I don't know what happened. One day we were friends, and the next day we weren't."

I hear plaintive, extensive searches for meaning behind a sense of great loss. Some friendships survive the loss of loves, family, jobs, locations . . . and others do not. Some friendships collapse at the first overload on their bridge.

Living boldly into a friendship does not come with a map or a set of instructions. It is as personal and complex as the people who are involved. There are ways to sharpen your pencil as you create the story.

"I remember," Gina told me, "that in Uganda when a friend stands in front of a friend they have a saying which means I am the mirror of your heart." What a sweet thought that is . . . that a friend on the kindest day reflects our goodnesses back to us and we to them.

I want every story to end with me reflecting the large and open(ing) hearts of my friends. I want there to be grand vision and intense longing for goodness to express itself in practical ways every moment. I reflect symbols for which we have no words, only movement and chant and enchanting dreams. I reflect to my treasured souls that they have the courage and dare to dream of the longings of their hearts . . . and I will support those dreams.

I will reflect the finest qualities my friends offer me and remind them of all the promise I see in them. Profound knowingness and curiosity.

May I always have the strength of love in my heart to tell a story from my heart to the heart of a friend.

My friend Tina gave me a magnet with a very important reminder on it: Do not pass on the opportunity to tell someone you love them. Such good advice. I pass it along.

· tool kit ·

Reward your friends. Honor them with an award for one of their strongest qualities. Or for a special moment that you have shared. Send them a shiny quarter, a two-dollar bill, a certificate, a sticker, a little pocket token. . . . Something physical that they can hold and treasure.

We often celebrate our friends to other people. If you have something good to say about a friend to someone else, make sure you tell your friend, too.

Reflect life patterns for your friends. Help them identify successful patterns that they may not notice in themselves.

play as often as you can

Healthy Choices

adjective. 1. in good health. 2. indicative of, conducive to, or promoting good health. 3. (of a person's attitude) sensible and well balanced.

Twenty years from now you will be more disappointed by the things that you didn't do than by the ones you did do. So throw off the bowlines. Sail away from the safe harbor. Catch the trade winds in your sails. Explore. Dream. Discover.

—Mark Twain

know the best and highest choices for health and most often choose those things.

—mar

Healthy Choices. I believe an entire frozen food line has been thus named. It's natural to associate these two words with food. When I was speaking in a grade school, I walked past an open schoolroom door. From the festive decorations on the classroom walls, I would say kindergarten or first grade. I saw a smiling instructor directing her active and interacting students, "Let's practice our healthy choices."

Let's practice our healthy choices. Beyond food. Movement. Of all kinds. From exercise to ergonomic positioning to physical awareness while in transit. The words we speak. The routes we take. The friends we choose. The entertainment we watch and participate in. Promotion of good health. The types of thoughts we bring to our mind on a regular basis. Our internal dialogue. The environment we build around ourselves.

All of us begin to define for ourselves what it is to make a healthy choice. Yet I see all around me people who associate with individuals who criticize them, promote negative thinking, and generally spin their world on a downward spiral. Still, those individuals are a choice in their life. A healthy choice?

Healthy choices thread through every aspect life. The key here, as in nearly every boldness which I take upon myself, is a heightened awareness. Tony Robbins and many other inspiring instructors talk about the process of creating a trigger to remind you of a desire to change a certain behavior. I was reminded of this practice in a journal-writing class I teach in a medium-security prison. The session was nearing the end. The curriculum had been covered, and we were having a last conversation. Casually I mentioned the need to remind myself of a new behavior we had all discussed.

"Rubber band," one of the participants said.

"What?"

"Put a rubber band on your wrist. When you go home tonight. Get one and put it on your wrist. And snap it. When you snap it . . . say that thing out loud. Then tomorrow do the same thing. Wear the rubber band until you remember."

I thanked him for the suggestion and asked him, "Does that work for you?"

Everybody in the class just howled. Slapped their legs and guffawed. "You think if it worked for him he'd be in here?"

Still my helper was adamant. "I didn't learn the rubber band deal until I got in here. It's helped me make a lot of positive changes. I just need some reminding. Maybe if I'd known this reminding trick when I was younger, I wouldn't be in here today."

I smiled. I said I would use the protocol. And I did. It helped. I made healthy choices. And after a few days, I took the rubber band off.

My students in the prison system have taught me a great deal about making healthy choices over the years. Not only are many of them highly motivated to change, to lean a different way in their lives, but so much consequence is riding on their choices. One unhealthy choice under supervision, and they can end up back in prison.

What kind of consequences can you create for yourself to motivate consistent healthy choices? Can you create consequences when you make changes inconsistent with your expressed bold desire? Who in your world demonstrates the skill of consistently making choices that seem clearly in their own best interests? Can you ask them how they make those decisions?

Wear a rubber band as a reminder of a choice you want to institute. Snap it!

Nurture

verb. 1. care for and encourage the growth or development of. 2. cherish (a hope, belief, or ambition). noun. 1. the process of caring for and encouraging the growth or development of someone or something. 2. upbringing, education, and environment.

What do we live for if it is not to make life less difficult for one another?

—George Eliot (aka Mary Anne Evans)

---

gardening is all about optimism. i put a seed in the ground. i consistently tend it, confident i will see the results, in time, of all the nurture i have provided.

—mar

The friends and family who touch your heart? Yes. They *know* you love them. True. But Mary Ann Evans, writing as George Eliot, pointed out that "Silence lasts long enough beyond the grave. If you would have words of love—then speak them now." Indeed. The whole "send flowers to the living" thing. There's merit in that.

My friend Jan sipped her coffee as we chatted through an afternoon get together. Our time was coming to a close because she still had to fit in a visit to a friend in the hospital.

Her cell phone rang. She checked the number and excused herself. When she returned to the table she wore a face of sadness and quietly told me one of her elder friends had died just that afternoon. He was in a hospice, in a great deal of pain. She was glad he no longer had to suffer.

I nodded. I just listened. Tears sat on the edges of her eyes as she explained, "Grief in loss is hard for anybody. I have faith in more than this life. But it doesn't mean that loss here is any easier. But here's what I know. I have no regrets. This afternoon's visit would have been just like Tuesday's visit. And the time before that. Every time I left Bill, I held his hand and I asked him if there was anything in the whole wide world I could get for him, or do for him. He always said no. I knew that just my being there was enough."

Bill was nurtured by Jan in his last days. She didn't bring him anything. She didn't do anything for him. She just showed up.

And in sitting with my friend's grief, the best comfort I could offer was to just let her tell her story.

Nurturing is not complex. It's simply being tuned in to the thing or person before you and offering small gestures toward what it needs at that time. I think of the phrase to give someone a "hand up." Not a ladder. Not a set of stairs. Not a whole airplane. Just a hand up. Nurturing is measured gestures in somewhat consistent fashion.

Nurturing is not always the same. What a seed needs when it is first planted is different than what it needs when it is further along in its growing. It requires a boldness in our seeing. A willingness to observe the true condition of what is before us and assessing the most appropriate action to contribute to the growth and wellness of that plant, that person.

· tool kit ·

The precious hearts in your life, the friends who are there for you no matter what, those whose hearts are connected to you over miles, over years . . . *how* would you like to pause to recognize them? How do you nurture them? What would create a treasured memory?

Make a list of all the reasons the relationships in your life are treasured, are precious to you. And then make your nurturing plan. Let that plan involve saying those things which are deeply understood but often do not get spoken out loud.

It is often true that people give what they wish to receive. Notice the ways important people in your life give to others. And try returning that gift to them as a way of nurturing them.

Recognize that nurturing yourself is as important (if not more so) as nurturing others. Identify some ways that you flourish under nourishing care. Provide them for yourself.

Movement

noun. act of changing actual location or position.

*We should consider every day lost in which we have not
danced at least once.*

—Friedrich Nietzsche

---

*i will dance a little. i will move with the wind. i will
give my body to my love and celebrate that we have
substance beyond the idea of ourselves. we can move.
we can touch. this is my physical exclamation point.
this is how i can awaken my mind to the possibilities
in the day.*

—mar

Movement energizes. There's plenty of material available to demonstrate the benefits of physical activity. Part of the trick for me is to make movement enjoyable. Actually, it's *most* of the trick for me. I have never been particularly fond of exercise. Even as an active youngster, when given a choice I picked reading a book over taking a hike. There's a humorous quote making its rounds: Every once in a while the urge to exercise comes upon me. If I just lie down, it usually passes.

When I want to be bold about my movement . . . I for sure do not call it exercise! I consider it dancing, and therefore, music and movement are a great combination for me. I dance. I walk and enjoy music as I'm walking. In this way, movement becomes yet another creative expression for me.

My husband rides his road bikes with a passion. He is informed and serious about his riding. In fact, he calls his rides "the long prayer." Movement on his bike keeps him connected to the important spiritual components of his life. In his life experience, movement is intimately tied to spirituality.

My friend Noah Singer is also a road racer. He's finishing up college and entering the world of professional racing. This is serious stuff. He keeps a blog, and when I look at some of the photos from the races, his face looks as if he is in pain. And, guess what? He is.

I wanted to pump up some of my own inspiration around movement. And, as is my practice when longing to live a certain thing with boldness, I went to someone who knows a lot about what I want to know. And I asked Noah three questions:

"What motivates you to MOVE when you don't feel like it?"

"If I am not motivated to move, I am probably sick, injured, or sleeping. As long as I can remember, I have been a pretty active and outdoorsy person. I have never understood how to get to the fireworks of victory in a video game or been an avid movie fan. Now that much of my life revolves around cycling, most of my days are spent hunched over the handlebars, staring at the white line on the highway or the rich soil of Arkansas bike trails. On the days that I feel like backing off, I think about my competition. They are out riding, lifting weights, or looking into other ways of gaining the edge that will make the difference for them. I think about how lucky I am that, for now at least, my most important task is to ride my bicycle. That's pretty fortunate and gets me off my butt."

"What draws you forward through the pain of those last feet in a race?"

"There is a something called 'finish line fever.' It's when you are nearing the last five or ten miles of a race and you feel you're close to the finish but won't make it. When I feel my forehead getting warm with that fever, I think about all the miles I have already ridden that day, all the days I have ridden that month, and all the months I have ridden that year. . . . All that effort will pay off in the final few minutes."

"What does *non-training* movement look like for you? What do you do that's physical for fun, when you're not thinking of training?"

"When not training traditionally, I like to go wakeboarding on the lake in the summer or ride my snowboard in the winter.

I am very injury-prone, so I try to limit my time with these, but it is a way to keep active and motivated in a world shared by other people with different skills."

By virtue of my passion and my occupation, I spend a great deal of time sitting and writing. I've introduced movement into the traditionally sedentary process. At my writing desk I have both a traditional chair and an exercise ball. Most of the time I sit on the exercise ball. It's excellent for my posture and (with proper training from a professional on a video) I use it to stretch out. I bounce on it. By providing movement during an intensely focused process, I increase my productivity and manage to slip in some movement, too.

· tool kit ·

What kind of movement brings you joy? Is there more you can learn about it? Can you find a consistent place for it in your life?

Dance a little. Put on headphones. Put on music you *know* you love. Music that makes you want to move. And just dance a little. Or try putting on a pair of headphones with your favorite music when you are doing a redundant task. And move a little while you are doing the task.

work as
smart as you
are able

challenge

noun. 1. the state or condition of being difficult.
2. dare, provocation. 3. test, questioning, dispute,
stand, opposition, confrontation. 4. problem,
difficult task, test, trial.

*It's not what you are; it's what you don't become that
hurts.*

—Oscar Levant

---

*the challenge before us is to savor the unknown and
delight in the taste of possibility.*

—mar

The less I take the difficulties of my life as personal affront, and the more I use them as an opportunity to learn and grow . . . the easier I sleep at night. Facing a difficulty requires a willingness of heart: a willingness to step away from the blinding effect of fear and simply look at the thing I am facing, as well as I am able, to see it for what it is.

I remember a time of extraordinary financial hardship. Not only did I have to move in with friends, but I needed to liquidate a large percentage of my belongings. While at the time it was a painful experience . . . I learned. In a systematic process, I really separated myself from the weight of so many things. I have the privilege of clarity into how insidious continual acquisition can become. Shopping can be fun. Acquiring and collecting is entertaining. When is enough—enough? This challenge helped me ask some very important questions.

I wrote on the day of my larger than life "estate" sale . . .

The goods sit. Piled. Disheveled. Cars come and go, carrying people in need and needy people—very few people come of true lack: those who do, leave with more than they paid for. Ah, everyone's leaving with more than they paid for. They just don't know it. Stories, history, longing, anniversary gifts intended to stand in for a love which no longer existed. Acquisitions came to my hand for beauty, for function, for filling a void for which I did not have a name. The sob that rises in my throat is not so much at seeing so much go, as at my sorrow at ever having so much to begin with. I remember proudly displaying "live simply that others may simply live," and I lived that way for a long time, close to the ground, hospitable, generous. How did I step into the complexity of owing and owning and acquiring so many things? It's less about my possessions being packed and carted into the world—I'm used to that process because people cart off my words and stories into the world every day—it's more about this sense of challenge, this dying and rising again. I have coordinated the process for others at their death—my father's estate was sold and meted out in this way.

I almost got hit in a crosswalk with the WALK signal four times this week. Whew. I'm glad there's a financial challenge behind this process, instead of my death. Although a couple of those cars brought that possibility dangerously close. This extraordinary letting go places an interesting burden on me. Intentional living is not optional. The lessons I take in this day have to remain with me. As my possessions march in procession to the world, may I cast my words to the spring dawn and celebrate the power of possessions that are intangible and more precious and profound.

What if I willfully put aside my anxiety and concerns and conduct myself as if I were not challenged, and the days not difficult? What if I lift my voice in song, what if I practice the lessons I am now learning; what if I behave in such a way as to lead myself to a more joyful place . . . and every time a reminder of lack, or absence of resource, presents itself . . . I am willing to see it as opportunity rather than obstacle? What if I call it challenge, rather than crisis? What if, at the end of a matter, I ask, "What will I learn from this to make me better?" Perhaps I can change the way I look at things today. Just today.

When I take a deep breath and do the difficult thing first; when my courage does not depend on the weather, the economic forecast, or the winds of whim; when I know the most significant elements in my days are laughter, learning, and applying my finest efforts to each endeavor—then, because of these things, each morning is a pleasure and every day passed is a success.

• tool kit •

This thing may challenge me, but it does not define me. I may learn from my challenges, but I do not identify who I am by the nature of the challenge I face.

Use the perspective of someone from the "Board of Director" exercise to offer you advice on how to manage through a challenge.

Pick up a stone that feels good to you and is small enough to hold in one hand. Consider how long that stone has been around and what enormous pressure it has experienced. Draw strength from its long history.

Relentless Commitment

relentless, adjective. 1. intensely constant; incessant. 2. harsh or inflexible, rigid. 3. continual, continuous, nonstop, never-ending, unabating, interminable, unceasing, endless, unending, unremitting, unrelenting, unrelieved. 4. unfaltering.

commitment, noun. 1. the act of committing or the state of being committed. 2. dedication, application. 3. a pledge or undertaking, obligation.

The country needs and, unless I mistake its temper, the country demands bold, persistent experimentation. It is common sense to take a method and try it. If it fails, admit it frankly and try another. But above all, try something.

—Franklin D. Roosevelt

stirred awake by the exquisite music of my own relentless commitment.

—mar

"Oh, you are *so* serious. Will you lighten up?"

I heard these words a lot when I was younger. I smile when I tell you that I hear them quite a bit even now. There are certain things in my life to which I am relentlessly committed. And, yes, it calls up those words "inflexible," "rigid."

I was talking to a contractor once in a coffee shop. He casually shared a fascinating piece of perspective with me. I was talking about how rigid so many people are, and I was extolling the virtues of flexibility.

He said he looks at the world through his experience as a contractor. He aptly pointed out that it takes all types of strengths, textures, and materials to make a good house. For some applications flexibility is a great trait. And the more flexible, the stronger the structure. But there are other applications that require absolute immovable rigidity. It's essential.

When he was done talking about building materials, he smiled. "I'll be the first one to admit that hanging with somebody with a rigid commitment to something can be downright uncomfortable. But chances are they're going to give me an opportunity to be involved in something. Or donate to something they believe in. And that's not always a bad thing."

My relentless commitment has led me on some pretty extraordinary journeys. It still does.

I have written ever since I was a wee lass. Writing was an essential part of my life experience. My early choices led me away from a college education, so earning my living as a writer seemed a greater challenge. I used my writing and creative skills in every job I took on. In all instances, writing was only a portion of my job. After fifteen years of using my skills in other people's endeavors, I created a company that allowed me to use my passion and skill for writing. Over two decades later I had created hundreds of products all based on my artwork and my passion for writing.

Writing was still only a portion of my "job." My relentless commitment to my writing life led me to reinvent the structures of my days. Now, the bulk of my days is committed to writing and my creative endeavors. The transition was not (nor is it still) a simple process. I did not reinvent my life all by myself—the support and commitment of my closest friends made it a cooperative effort.

The transition came with uncertainty and pain, but the results speak of the boldness of my commitment. I remember a phrase I wrote many years ago: "An 'always been' doesn't mean I must choose 'what must be.'" My relentless commitment to writing has me standing places that long ago seemed simply a dream.

What are you committed to, relentlessly? When you identify what you always say "yes" to, it's easier to say "no" to other things.

The Legacy of Paul Wellstone
(inspired by Andrea Bidelman)

what is a legacy and how do we live into it?
a legacy is built upon
daily decisions recognizing the "small stuff"
isn't always.

a legacy is a reflection
of the integrity applied to
all circumstances.

a legacy is first a gift
which is given to the individual and then it
is a generosity of spirit sewn in a global garment.

we live daily into the path of a grand legacy. . . .
and we are inspired by such tall commitment and
    accomplishment.

share your heart
as deeply as
you can reach

Balance

noun. 1. an even distribution of weight enabling someone or something to remain upright and steady. 2. stability of one's mind or feelings. 3. a condition in which different elements are equal or in the correct proportions. 4. an apparatus for weighing. 5. a counteracting weight or force.

Progress might have been all right once, but it has gone on too long.

—Ogden Nash

---

life is defined more by its contrasts than its samenesses; life is defined more by its risks than the many securities.

—mar

As a teenager, balance struck me as meaning "the elements are in equal proportions." As I have grown up, I have come to see balance more in the context of elements being in "correct proportions." I become amused when I see or hear advertisements that talk about a "balanced life." As if there is a recipe for that. And thinking of recipes . . . rarely do all ingredients in a recipe's instruction come in equal distribution. There will at times be a lot more of one ingredient than the other. But that doesn't make the thing you are creating unbalanced. It just means the ingredients are in the appropriate proportion.

As I consider this metaphor for balance, I like to think of all the ingredients found in a typical kitchen. Not all elements will be used at all times, and certainly not in equal measure. But taken as a whole, the ingredients in the kitchen create the opportunity for balance. For they are available for immediate use when needed. And perhaps, in a period of time, the bulk of ingredients will have been used in equal measure—or, at least, appropriate measure. One wouldn't really want to use equal amounts of saffron to paprika, or cardamom to cayenne. Balance comes in knowing the correctness of the proportion.

My husband's doctor delivered the results of his cholesterol test with serious concern. My husband wanted to try and correct the "imbalance" nutritionally before choosing a medication approach. We went through the kitchen together, holding all of our kitchen ingredients up to the light of healthy cholesterol levels. We made a lot of changes that day.

Months have passed since that day, and now, writing of balance in regard to kitchen ingredients prompted a visit to our shelves. Boy, was I surprised—the correct proportions had taken a significant dive! I laughed right out loud, and I smiled that I had the opportunity to boldly step into balance today. I recycled what I could. Prepared to pass along what I could to folks in our community perhaps less concerned about cholesterol levels than we. Certainly we must consider the impact of the weight of a counterbalance. Any gymnast will tell you that balance on a beam isn't about rigidity but fluidity and flexibility. Ah. Balance.

I hear many people talk about their longing for a balanced life. What I think they are really expressing is a desire for a life with less pressure. A life with fewer demands pressing their noses against the windowpane of their day. But when does that happen? It happens for me when I make it happen. When I invite it to happen with my intentional actions and my guided perspective.

Think of the fourth definition of balance: an apparatus for weighing. Look at the components and elements of *your* day, week . . . any activity . . . and weigh them. Weigh them in the context of your mission. Your passion. Your priorities. That's how you see if they are in balance with the whole of your life. Or not. Most certainly, balance in appropriate measure can happen any time. All the time.

If balance isn't about perfect equilibrium, then how do you measure balance in your life? If balance is about appropriate proportions, then how do you determine when things are out of balance?

Rotarians have what they call their "Four-Way Test." It consists of four questions by which they encourage their members to assess their thoughts, words, and actions and make balanced decisions. They are:

1. Is it the TRUTH?
2. Is it FAIR to all concerned?
3. Will it build GOODWILL and better friendships?
4. Will it be BENEFICIAL to all concerned?

Create your own set of questions to test the balance of your life.

Family

noun. 1. a group living together in a household.
2. a group of people related to one another by
blood or marriage. 3. a person or people related
to one and so to be treated with a special loyalty.

*There is no doubt that it is around the family and the
home that all the greatest virtues, the most dominating
virtues of human society, are created, strengthened and
maintained.*

—Winston Churchill

---

fate makes us family. choice makes us friends.
    there are two lines
    i fill out with your name:
    nearest relative and
    person to call in case of emergency.

that i was born to this circle—i am blessed.
that i choose to stand in this circle—i am proud.

—mar

As my father began to confront the realities of his impending Alzheimer's disease, he asked me to dispose of the bulk of his belongings. I did so in the manner in which he instructed me. My oldest brother took aggressive exception to this. These two had been estranged, and yet there were possessions that had value to my brother. Angry and full of a childhood of unresolved issues, my brother phoned me. He was threatening and expected quite a bit of resistance from me. He received none. I asked him to list the items that were most important to him. He did. I told him I'd call him back in two days. I did. I tracked down the two items to which he had attached importance. I redeemed them from their new homes.

We arranged the time for him to pick them up. My father offered only a little objection. It went easier for him as I explained that this was really to make life easier for me.

My coworker Elizabeth helped me see this relationship with my brother in an entirely new way. Elizabeth pointed out that a lot of people accept their family by default. She explained that her family ties were made stronger because she had actively chosen each one of them. She did not merely accept the dictates of blood but recognized that family went beyond blood. That explanation changed the way I saw family.

The day my brother came to claim his items, we took the chance to speak some calm words to each other. It was healing for both of us. As my brother readied for his long drive home, he thanked me for making "this thing" possible. I told him I wanted the last thing I did with him to be a positive experience.

And then I said, "Let's face it, neither one of us would choose each other's company if we were strangers. So now we can be free from trying to choose each other just because we are related by blood." We both understood that this was good-bye. It was the last time I saw my brother. A few years later, he too left the planet due to illness.

My family consists of many people who are of my bloodline. There are more people in my family circle with whom I share a line of value and intention. And they are every bit my family. I create traditions with them and would do anything for them. My family continues to grow.

Family shows up in your life at entirely unexpected times. And family doesn't always look like you. Family can have different skin color and speak with an accent different from your own. But you recognize a family member because they can tease you mercilessly and you don't take it personally. You can appear in your worst clothes and family will tell you you look great—and you believe them.

Dr. Lenis Whalen has been practicing chiropractic medicine in Florida for over twenty years. I've observed, over time, that he expands his family by allowing his friends into his "tribe." This is what he has to say about family:

> When people ask me who are my best friends, my answer
>   is easy
> I grew up with them.
> They are my brothers and sisters.
> The term is family.

As I age the more I realize
not only how fortunate I was to grow up in this tribe
but how fortunate to have the parents I did. . . .
they guided us with the lessons that they learned.
To honor them we are continuing that legacy.

· **tool kit** ·

what is our family?
look below us: our history is the
foundation beneath us.

what is our family?
we look across the table and see the
hands of friends holding us firmly.

what is our family?
we consider our livelihood and know
these structures provide security and
makes us stronger and smarter.

what is our family?
we hear the laughter and know our children
will teach us more than we will ever teach them.

what is our family?
we touch our full hearts and see ourselves
reflected whole in each other's eyes.

Do you choose your family? Do you consider members of your family as friends? Are there people whom you consider family who are not related to you by blood? Have you experienced estrangement from family, and could you build a bridge if you wanted to? Conversely, is there someone from whom you should step away? Have there been people in your life who have fulfilled family-like roles? Have you acknowledged them as family? How do you define family, and how do you remember and honor them?

choose in ways
that support
your dreams

Change

verb. make or become different, transform.
noun. the act or instance of making or
becoming different.

Things do not change; we change.

—Henry David Thoreau

---

goes the song, "we change, we change."
but the music is still mine.
change of any sort requires courage.

—mar

My friend Mike Wigal has encountered much change in the last three years. He lost his wife and lifelong friend to cancer. He switched jobs. He started traveling and establishing a list of "must see" places. He created a blog and decided to "make the best of what's left." He is going through the long application to serve in the Peace Corps. I asked him what he had to say about change. His response both inspires me and makes me smile. He said . . .

There is *so* much to say about change. It's the flip side of the coin from "control." Change keeps us from going stale. Helps prevent Alzheimer's. Excites us. Teaches us. Inspires us. Creates us.

In our lives, we are either growing or shrinking. There is no such thing as "maintaining." Embracing change willfully means we develop our ability to adapt to new situations, new environments, both expected and unexpected. Change will come to our lives. Friends will come and go. Jobs will be lost. Children will leave the nest. Loved ones will die. How we adapt, how we deal with those changes determines how well we live our lives.

What does not destroy us makes us stronger! (Nietzsche) Yet I still like to have my toothbrush in the same spot every morning.

—Mike Wigal

As I was exercising this morning, I remembered something my friend Andy said: Love and doing some good—the two things that weigh in for him at the end of the day. And then I thought of a conversation with a client, Carole, who asserted that peace isn't a condition but a destination. It's not someplace we can arrive at, it's a desire, a place to which we are continually traveling.

I turned off my exercise music, found my journal, and wrote:

no kudos here, kid.
just another cold, misty morning inviting,
"want to go again?"

to the road. to the mat.
to the ring. to the field. to the board.
i go. i go to do what i know. and maybe on this road
i add in a little nourishment, some "tucker" for myself
and others. a little something that's new and beyond what
    i know.

will there be declarations?
a revolution? illuminations?
no. probably not.

but maybe some time today i
can set my loving heart
down on some unloved square
and move a piece that makes
a difference on the board.
maybe i can take one step
on that profoundly complex
path to peace.

and tonight, late, when i'm still not
done with the day but must comply
with sleep, i can whisper,
"there was done a little good today.
today i changed myself and the world,
just a little.
and yes, i loved."

most days, that is enough.

• tool kit •

Just stop it. Seriously. Whatever it is. Just stop
it. If only for an hour, a day, or a week. Stop
doing it long enough to get a glimpse of what the
change would actually look like.

What happens when I am willing to accept change
more readily, without resistance? What is it about
sameness that so draws me, and how could I begin to
have that kind of attraction to change?

Priorities

noun. 1. a thing that is regarded as more important than another. 2. the fact or condition of being regarded or treated as more important. 3. the right to take precedence or to proceed before others.

Even if you are on the right track, you will get run over if you just sit there.

—Will Rogers

---

choose the whole of your environment, things and events, based upon the value, meaning, and function they hold. do not allow obligation or immediacy to bind you to physical things or specific actions.

—mar

It is a better thing to weigh and measure priorities in the illuminating light of your own mission than to have your activities formed by the impressions and expectations of others.

I've been privileged to be near several dear souls as they have prepared to enter the world of dying. There is so much to be learned about priorities in this time. There's an unattributed saying: "No one ever is heard to say on their deathbed, 'I wish I had worked at the office more.'"

In the press of life's many tasks and obligations, one's priorities can become skewed. Years ago, as I was preparing to leave from my extended stay in Paris, I was under the impression that I would be coming back in a few months. Not so. I wrote later, "If I had known it was to be my last time in Paris, I would have lingered over my coffee a little longer." We can choose, repeatedly, the laundry or dishes over the moment of play with a child. The walk outdoors may be set aside in favor of completing a marketing strategy, organizing a cupboard, or any number of other professional or domestic activities. When I choose to introduce the "live as if this is all there is" philosophy into my day, my choices become different.

This is not advocacy for hedonism. This is instead a plea for creating memories that are rich and full, and recognizing that at the end of our lives we may remember our friendships and sunny walking afternoons more than an elaborate report or well-organized closet. And those end-of-life memories don't just arrange themselves in a single day. Our daily decisions create the scrapbook of our life. I remember the sadness on the face of a grandmother I know who spent all afternoon cleaning her granddaughter's house, when all her granddaughter wanted to do was play with her grandma. A viewing of *The Wizard of Oz* will demonstrate that even Auntie Em was sad about the priority she chose of moving those chicks out of a broken incubator when Dorothy was nowhere to be found.

But setting priorities is tricky business. Because sometimes the chicks *have* to be moved. And in certain settings, the closet getting organized truly *is* the most significant thing. There's a koan that asserts, "The one who is too good at shooting does not hit the center of the target." And conversely, Thoreau said that men basically hit what they aim at.

So I should be clear on what I am good at, and make sure it is aligned with my apparent priorities. Oh, what power our experiences have when our skills and talents line up with what we want, in small or large scope. Essentially this speaks to intention, to our goal (center of the target) versus our distractions (our ability to shoot). Aim is more significant than shooting skill. Throughout the day I do a check-in with myself: Is this shooting? Or aim? I focus on the differences between being a good shooter and hitting the center of the target. I ask myself throughout the day, "What am I aiming at in this one day?" When I offer an honest response . . . amazing results ensue.

Talented people can confuse themselves with their profound and diverse shooting skills. Exercising those skills feels so satisfying, and it masquerades as productivity. Whereas the real significance in the day is measured by how close a shot is to target/center. Shooting skills, metaphorically, become a dangerous distraction. I say out loud, several times in a day, "Just because I *can* do it does not mean I *should* do it."

Then, of course, there are those days when the priority is actually developing our diverse shooting skills! Just got to have the focus to stay connected to whatever you have identified as your priorities.

• tool kit •

Look at the life of someone you know who seems to conduct their life with a balance of accomplishment and friendship, who achieves landmark projects but always seems to have time for a cuppa something or a little chat. This person *never* answers the question, "How are you?" with, "I'm swamped. I have *so* much to do." Because they are clear on their priorities. And they do not allow themselves to be defined by their busy-ness. They don't even allow themselves to be defined by their outcomes. Do you know someone like that? Ask them a few questions about how they establish their priorities. Apply that behavior and model that in your day.

as you hold
many possibilities
   measure your action against
   this question . . .
how will i like to remember this day?

and then,
the chosen answer becomes
your natural priority or "possibility."

honor your actions as your teachers

forgiveness

noun. the action or process of forgiving or being forgiven.

Forgive your enemies but never forget their names.

—John Fitzgerald Kennedy

i rest in the light of forgiveness. i forgive myself and others for that which is done (and better left undone) and also that which is not done (and better if done).

—mar

Forgiveness does not rest in the hands of anyone else. And it is not dependent upon anyone else. I'm not even sure forgiveness has anything to do with anyone else. It's not a matter of whether someone deserves it, or if they will even know about it. Forgiveness has to do with the burden I carry around. The load I'm hefting on the back of my heart. Forgiveness enables me to set the weight down. To not haul all the "how could you?" kinds of questions around. I wrap the potential for bitterness, resentment, martyrdom in the blanket of forgiveness and just set it down. Then it all just melts in the warmth. And goes away.

My husband and I decided that since so many of our dear friends had traveled great distances to be with us for our wedding, we would depart from the traditional concept of a honeymoon in favor of savoring time with them. So, the day after my wedding, some of my best girlfriends and I were traveling for the day. I started talking about mothering . . . having driven my groom's mother for 172 minutes to our wedding ceremony, just the day before. Maybe it was just 170 minutes. It seemed like 172. It was my first long visit with the woman who was about to become my mother-in-law.

She had mentioned that as an academic, she took comfort in the fact that she could study just about anything and experience some level of mastery. And yet, she produced two children and found virtually no viable instruction available to her on how to mother. Or be a good mother. After much conversation, she faltered and said to me, "I didn't know any better than to do what I had seen done." And then she spent a bit telling me how she came to hate her own mother. She didn't mention any forgiveness on the horizon.

My friend Connie said she understood those sentiments. That her experience was different, however, in that she had pledged to herself *not* to do what her mother had done. She couldn't remember how old she was when she decided she would forgive her mother for the host of her difficult actions in Connie's childhood. But she did forgive. And she credits the freedom that forgiveness gave her with her ability to be creative in the way she chose to raise her own children.

In one way or another, each woman in that car echoed the sentiment that forgiveness, dispensed with trueness, provides a significant lift and elevation to the daily life experience.

The process of extending forgiveness begins and ends within me. Even if I never connect with the object of my forgiveness, that doesn't change the outcome of my action of forgiveness.

Write a letter to the person to whom you want to extend forgiveness. Make it as long as you need it to be. When you are done, let it sit for a while. Walk away from it. Come back to it in a day, or a week. Read it out loud. Make any changes that time has provided the perspective to make. Then, tear the letter up and throw it away. It's done. You don't need the letter around. In fact . . . it's important to throw it away. Because that's what forgiveness does. It puts it behind you.

JFK said it well, and this exercise demonstrates it: Forgiveness allows the freedom of healing. Remembering allows the opportunity to not repeat the incident.

Reward

noun. 1. a thing given in recognition of service, effort, or achievement. 2. a fair return for good or bad behavior. 3. something offered for the detection of a criminal, the restoration of lost property, or the giving of information.

> *The highest reward for a person's toil is not what they get for it, but what they become by it.*
>
> —John Ruskin

> *the reward must be taken from the action, the thing itself.*
>
> —mar

Reward is both an internal and an external process. One without the other isn't compete. It requires insight to offer reward to yourself, and grace to accept it from others.

I wrote a phrase, "Pick the rose which you planted within yourself so long ago." I was in discussion with an individual whose external reward system was limited. We had a talk about how important it is to look to ourselves first, for reward. For consequence. For inspiration. "The person in the mirror" really is the first and last word. Praise from others is a luxury. It is a fine gift. But fundamentally the satisfaction has to come first from within.

As I look behind me at Judah, my Labrador, I wonder about this process as I write it. My willful Judah, with his large frame and large personality, has been trained by my husband. I should say "retrained." He sits behind me. Well behind me. Not in my way. Not under my feet or under the table, as he used to do. But kindly out of the way.

I turn and speak his name. He waits to be called.

"Here, Judah. Come here." He does. I scratch him behind the ears. I tell him he's the best dog in the world. I wish I could ask him if the new and good behavior he's demonstrating is satisfying to him. The answer comes from my common sense. He's a Labrador. After food, approval and affection are the two highest motivating factors in his life. And he gets those through his good behavior. And after a few weeks of some pretty difficult retraining protocols, he seems like a happier and more content dog. He knows what to do to be rewarded. But is the behavior reward in itself? And is it fair to compare my motivation to my dog's? Scientists have.

In a small drawer in one of my writing desk organizers, I keep a beautifully bound small book, smaller than a business card. Two of my best pals, a brother and sister, Gen and Ben, gifted me with it for my birthday years ago. Both of their ages were counted in single digits then, but they loved me lots bigger than their age. And they knew how much I love books.

That lovingness felt like a reward in itself. And that started me thinking. Maybe this tiny, precious book could be a receptacle for unexpected rewards. Words from others that bring my sights up. So when I am unable to reach into myself, and pull a reward from my own knowing, I can look in this book. I've kept precious rewarding words in this book for years. Comments from strangers, family, friends and associates, and clients are written small on the pages. These comments, these word rewards, serve me better than trophies, certificates, citations, or honorary degrees. They are rewards issued sincerely, spontaneously, from the heart of the speaker. And over time, they have become a giant body of incentive. *Reward* in the truest sense.

When the wizard handed the tin man his heart, he made a statement that I both understand and struggle to grasp: "Remember, a heart is not judged by how much it loves but by how much it is loved by others."

This is a paradox. I am willing to live with it. I believe love exists wholly in its act of being given. And then, there's that other thing. The reciprocity. The acceptance of the gift, which seems to complete it or make it whole. I wish I could write that I can reconcile this neatly and tie it in a beautiful package. Can't. That's why we have a word like paradox.

My young friend Taylina was discussing the puzzling impact of apparently same things that are actually totally different. And yet . . .

I told her that was a paradox.

"A pair of what?"

I thought for a moment and said, "Remember it this way. 'A pair of ducks.' One dressed in plaid. One in paisley. They contradict, but they are the same. That is a pair of ducks that is a paradox."

We laughed. I smiled at her long, drawn-out question, "Whaaat?"

I was thinking in paradox. Small child and Supreme Court justice. The small matters of her child-days contrasted to the growing sense of world stimulated by investigating complex concepts such as paradox. And I took reward from that.

Taylina, my friend, is in my reward book. When I returned from a long trip, she drew a card with a beautiful rainbow on it. Trained her whole lifetime to understand the process of greeting cards . . . she added text to accompany the illustration. She told me, "You are the pot (of gold) at the end of every rainbow."

Emerson said that if a person has won the affection of children . . . then they have succeeded. In the boldness of my own reward system, I feel quite successful.

· tool kit ·

To laugh often, to win the affection of children, to earn the appreciation of honest critics and endure the betrayal of false friends, to appreciate beauty, to find the best in others, to leave the world a bit better, whether by a healthy child, a garden patch . . . to know even one life has breathed easier because you have lived. This is to have succeeded.

—Ralph Waldo Emerson

Go to any thrift store or secondhand store and look for a small trophy. Or a recognition plaque. Bring it home and make little plaques to cover up the words that are printed there. Change them as you need recognition or reward for something you have done. Provide yourself the reward. Put it on the mantel. Seriously.

Start a small book. When you are acknowledged, rewarded, honored, or recognized in a way that feels exceptional, record it. When you are affirmed or validated in a particularly helpful way, record that. Use this record as a resource when you feel unseen or lacking support.

as you

awaken

Illumination

noun. 1. lighting or light. 2. a display of lights on a building
or other structure. 3. spiritual or intellectual enlightenment.

*What is life? It is the flash of a firefly in the night. It is
the breath of a buffalo in the wintertime. It is the little
shadow which runs across the grass and loses itself in
the sunset.*

—Crowfoot (last words, 1890)

---

*i awakened. is that not a wonderful statement? i
awakened, i no longer slept. every cell of my being is
illuminated by this dawn. i drew up the shades of my
spirit and gazed upon the vitality of life. i awakened.*

—mar

What is it that comes knocking on the door of my thinking self when I think I am sleeping? I am sleeping. But this visitor is of the opinion I should be awake. Awake as well as dreaming. Is that the firefly of illumination?

Illumination is a result of questions formed, continued questioning, and a synthesizing of available information, actual experience, and some things that I just make up. All those meet in a confluence, a bend in the river of my life, and create an insight. Like a lightning strike, it comes upon me quickly. And it doesn't seem to be built on the foundation of anything (although, of course, it is).

Someone unfamiliar with this firefly might say rather, "It suddenly dawned on me. . . ." Illumination is a quick dawn. The rising of our own sun within the day of our understanding. But clarity likes to visit me around three in the morning. Initially I'm not particularly pleased with the visit . . . since I was pretty busy sleeping. Enjoying the full, worked-up-to-it, all-night deep sleep that I need to feel really rested. And here comes clarity, charging into my slumber with something that's going to heighten the quality of my life. I wake up. I get it.

Some people like to call illumination an "aha!" moment. It's that significant instant when what has been unclear becomes clear. Or that which has been a struggle becomes a matter of ease. We all know that "being in the dark" represents some level of *not* understanding. Illumination casts its wonderful light on any subject and voilà—there is comprehension. Synthesis. "*Oh. I get it.*"

At a deeper level . . . illumination can be that one thing that is the passionate motivator of my actions. The light that comes shining out from within. The thing that, when I am doing it, I feel most invigorated. Most rewarded. Some people might call it knowing your life purpose. I call it your one illuminating thing. When you know what *that* is, it can shine light on almost any difficulty or challenge. And it can make the good and fine times the best and finest times. This is an elusive combination of personal light, clarity, and insight.

• tool kit •

When do you feel most invigorated? Most alive? What actions do you long to repeat because they feel so rewarding? Take note of these things. They may be your illuminating things . . . or lead you to them.

Presence

noun. the state or fact of existing, occurring, or being present in a place or thing.

We want to live in the present, and the only history that is worth a tinker's dam is the history we make today.

—Henry Ford

---

be present to your own spirit: listen. embrace your convictions without apology. whisper as the rain. laugh thunderously. speak your "yes" firmly. overwhelm your sorrows with action. create a day you will long remember.

—mar

My brother-in-law and I laughed heartily. He and my sister had driven the forty-five minutes from their home to my home. And he said he was almost in my town before he noticed where he was. The whole trip had compressed into an unnoticed ball. We made appropriate comments about how it was a good thing he noticed where he was before he passed the exit . . . or something more dramatic happened. That's happened to me, too.

Jan Johnson, publisher of Conari Press, talks about presence as "Being where you are, doing what you're doing, when you're doing it." Our culture's habit of celebrating multitasking goes counter to this. But more and more people are talking about the true productivity of fully focusing on one thing, utterly and completely.

I can remember talking to a Buddhist practitioner about this very thing. He said that multitasking was a sign of not being present to the moment. The more you begin to not notice where you are, or become multifocused . . . the more you are absent. Or not present.

If I had to pick a synonym for presence I would say "attentiveness" is close. But presence is even bigger than that. Living fully. Expanding to the edge of my own borders, my own skin. Listening hard. Being respectful of the matters at hand and reining my thinking in from last week, and twenty minutes ago, and what I'm going to do five minutes from now, and tomorrow.

We've all had it happen to us. We're having a conversation with a friend, and it suddenly dawns on us that they aren't really present to us. For whatever reason, their mind and attention are on matters other than the conversation at hand. It's like that trumpet sound that the Charlie Brown cartoons use to represent adults talking: Wha-wha-whahhhhh-wha. No words. Just sound. When presence is really lost—there isn't even any sound.

Presence requires an internal alertness to the all and everything immediately surrounding us.

• tool kit •

How does losing presence happen? More importantly, how do you keep it from happening repeatedly? What does it look like to my friend when I am not present to the moment? And how does it feel to me?

Get an egg timer. Turn it over when you are beginning one single task. Hold yourself accountable to only do that one thing until the timer has run out. Do not answer the phone or check e-mail. Be present. Practice presence.

Carry something with you in your pocket or in your hand. Let it be a physical reminder (icon) of being present to the experience you are entering. If you practice this enough times, all you'll have to do is think of this object and it will remind you to practice presence.

may your dreams
greet you
by name

Celebration

noun. 1. the action of marking one's pleasure at an important event or occasion by engaging in enjoyable, typically social, activity. 2. party, gathering, festivities, festival, fête, carnival, gala, jamboree, function. 3. commemoration, observance, performance, officiation, solemnization.

The more you praise and celebrate your life, the more there is in life to celebrate.

—Oprah Winfrey

celebration wears a lot of different outfits but always wears the same old, beautiful dancing shoes.

—mar

We call her the Queen of Celebration. There are even people in my friend Barbara Anne's life who don't know her official title, yet they understand that things are quite a bit more festive when she is around. Even Barbara Anne's personal gatherings are celebrations. She doesn't just have a buffet gathering—she hosts an event. With music. And speeches. Presentations. Fanfare. Decorations. Her celebrations are orchestrations and become incredible and cherished memories for those who participate.

In her business life, she adds a spirit of celebration to meetings. "Well, we finished that agenda *five* minutes ahead of schedule. Good for us!"

When a project is completed, or awarded. When someone is promoted. When someone retires. When someone arrives. Every transition, every thing that marks a shift for the better, toward positive change, deserves its own celebration. From making small note of it to having a glorious event about or around it.

A spirit of celebration allows one to notice things that may pass under other eyes as simply ordinary. Seeing the extraordinary is a gift of celebration. Celebration creates a sense of legacy and memory. It acknowledges that even on seemingly ordinary days, significant transitions occur, and we are able to acknowledge them.

in our journey, in the eloquent moments of each day, i seek celebration of the small graces and offer up the prayer of the small. it is of the small joys and little pleasures that the greatest of our days are built.

it's a celebration, a holiday of grand proportion, the day we chose to name each other, "friend."

—mar

Look for ways in this day to commemorate transitions, accomplishments, and completed endeavors. Introduce a new element into the process of creating acknowledgment. Welcome a spirit of festivity and embrace the extraordinary in what may appear rather ordinary.

Create

verb. 1. bring (something) into existence. 2. cause
(something) to happen as a result of one's actions. (Late
Middle English, in the sense *form out of nothing*.)

*Life does not consist mainly—or even largely—of facts
and happenings. It consists mainly of the storm of
thoughts that is forever blowing through one's head.*

—Mark Twain

*possibilities gather in the dark, light a candle and
imagine the day which tomorrow may create.*

—mar

Picasso. What a wonder. What a scoundrel. When I think of Pablo Picasso, I immediately both smile and shake my head. I bet he loved humming, "I did it my way." He certainly did. There was no snobbery involved in the components of his work. Every element from everyday life was fair game for art. It seemed certain to me, as I wandered about the museums dedicated to his life and work, both in Paris and in the Côte d' Azur, that his natural curiosity prompted him to look at almost everything with the question beginning, "What if . . . ?" on his lips. An expression I've treasured since I learned it was attributed to him is, "If I knew what it was going to be before I made it, why would I bother?"

As I consider the lives of my many friends who have birthed children, this makes a great deal of sense. Yes. They are very clear that there is going to be a child, but the way of being of that child is a mystery. And—I must laugh—it is more of a mystery to some parents than to others!

Create. To create. Something from nothing. This is frequently associated with art, but it applies to everything. You have heard someone assess, "She makes project management (or fill in the blank) an art form." Creating an effective and accessible plan for a project is an art form. To Create. Something from nothing.

How can I redefine what it means to create? What is it I would look like were I to create? Or if I called myself creative. What are some simple ways I can introduce creative processes into my home, into my workplace?

and may
you answer
"yes"

Enthusiasm

noun. 1. intense and eager enjoyment, interest, or approval.
2. eagerness, keenness, ardor, fervor, passion, zeal, zest,
gusto, energy, verve, vigor, vehemence, fire, spirit, avidity.
3. wholeheartedness, commitment, willingness, devotion,
earnestness.

Nothing great was ever achieved without enthusiasm.
—Ralph Waldo Emerson

---

begin each day as if it were on purpose.

—mar

If I am a toy with movable parts, enthusiasm is the battery that makes me move. If I am a vehicle, enthusiasm is the fuel. If my life is a beautifully crafted piece of stained glass, enthusiasm is the light shining through that highlights all the details.

With enthusiasm applied to any endeavor, I am more likely to come to it with a commitment toward completing it, come up with new ideas, and experience joy in it, in spite of myself.

I remember telling a friend years ago that I tried to not get out of bed until I could muster some level of enthusiasm for the day. He laughed so hard, and said, "I don't think anyone would see me until mid-afternoon if I waited for enthusiasm to get out of bed." Then, when we had finished laughing, this made me sad—and even now as I think back on it, it still does.

In corporate life, enthusiasm is saved by some executives like a secret weapon. For many people in the workforce, enthusiasm is reserved for one's personal life. Enthusiasm only shows up in the workplace when the conversation turns to the end of the workday.

My turn at the coffee counter. I greet the barista. "How are you today?" I am informed that he will be great in two hours and fifteen minutes, when work is over.

"Why?"

He looks at me in that sort of way that adults reserve for children who earnestly ask the most obvious questions. Almost patronizingly, he informs me of what he is sure I should already know: "In two hours and fifteen minutes, my work shift will be over and I can start doing things I really care about."

It only took me two seconds to wish him a good day and be on my way. I wanted my coffee brewed by someone who cared about what they were doing. I didn't want to have to order, "One Americano with cream and a generous portion of enthusiasm, please." Nor did I want to drink a beverage prepared by hands so clearly uninterested in the process.

Conversely, when I was shopping at a national pharmacy chain, a gentleman in a corporate uniform approached me and asked if I needed help. He took the goods I was holding and said he'd keep them at the counter for me. As I thanked him, I noticed he limped somewhat as he walked. When he was back behind the counter, facing me, I saw that his face was scarred and he was disfigured. Ah. But his smile lit up as he saw me approaching.

"Did you enjoy your experience shopping with us today?"

Well, yes I did, and I told him so.

"That just makes me so happy. I want you to keep coming back, and if there's anything we can do to help you be a more satisfied customer—you just let me know."

His enthusiasm made me believe he would personally tend to my satisfaction. And his smile overcame the impact any physical impairment might have. I took note of the time of day, because if I needed to shop here again soon, I wanted to come when this gentleman was working. His enthusiasm was the bright light shining through the stained glass of his personality.

If you want to see the embodiment of enthusiasm, go to a barbershop quartet practice, jam session, or competition anywhere in the world. Or watch a performance of Sweet Adelines, the female version of barbershop music. Those singers have elevated enthusiasm to an art form. They love to sing. Music just has a way of lighting up around them like fireworks. They can't stand still. Even when someone from a quartet is just talking about music, not even singing, they cannot still that enthusiasm. And why would they want to? That fuel, that battery pack that lights them up, spills into all areas of their life. I've seen it in young and old, male and female, and all shapes and sizes. Enthusiasm. It's contagious. From one aspect of a person's life to another and also from one person to another.

I enjoyed working with a very talented young woman named Amanda. Her customer service skills were extraordinary. Every time she spoke on the phone she had a smile in her voice and on her face. I asked her about it one day—because I noticed that she didn't always have a smile on her face when she was speaking in person. She explained she'd learned at one of her first jobs that it's very difficult to be unpleasant to someone on the phone when you are wearing a smile. And our customers agreed that her service was cheerful, welcoming, and . . . enthusiastic! The more difficult a customer might be, the bigger smile she'd wear.

How can I take enthusiasm that I experience about certain things in my life and apply that to other areas that do not much motivate me? What does enthusiasm look like on me when it occurs naturally? When I think of the most enthusiastic person I know . . . who is it? What are the qualities they demonstrate when they are being enthusiastic?

Pay attention to what happens to you when you are genuinely enthusiastic about something. How do you feel? Notice your gestures and how you move your body. Does your speaking pattern change—or the tone of your voice?

Think of one task about which you have been reluctant and step into it modeling those characteristics of enthusiasm. See if it makes you feel different about the outcome. Try Amanda's approach: smile on the phone when you are dealing with a difficulty. See if it makes a difference.

Question

noun. a sentence worded or expressed so as to elicit information.

It is better to ask some of the questions than to know all of the answers.

—James Thurber

---

it is not the easy or convenient life for which i search but life lived to the edge of all my possibility.

—mar

On certain days the questions vastly outweigh the answers.

To live boldly with questions frees me from having to know everything in a moment. How do I start that questioning journey? How to step beyond the reporters' questions of Who? What? When? Where? And why? Or how? Perhaps with a forgiving pen, writing under a wide sky with true light. In the writing we discover the difference between being uncertain and questioning, between taking risks and being at risk . . . the remarkable friendship between what is actual and what is possible. In lifting your pen you begin to write your way into the best questions of your life.

In his *Letters to a Young Poet,* Rainer Maria Rilke suggested that, rather than being wedded to the answers, we must come to a place where we actually love the questions themselves. The questions, on their own, give insight into whatever the puzzle may be. And Rilke does allow that, someday, it will come about that we will walk with all our questions and just live right into the answers. I treasure that sentiment.

The art of asking questions is much like peeling an onion down to its smallest sphere. Layer by layer the truthful and penetrating questions work the thing down to a core.

I've seen the most effective managers use questions in incredibly creative ways. Just a straightforward, "What do you think we should do?" generates unexpected, inventive possibilities. If a manager just chose to provide an answer, they'd be missing a clear opportunity for innovation. The well-timed question is more impacting than an answer.

· tool kit ·

Here's a condensed version of a journal exercise I teach. It works well to develop the art of questioning.

Take any quandary. One that has an immediate impact on some aspect of your life. Use your journal. Or plain paper. A keyboard. However it is that you best like to write. (And the more you write through these things, the easier it is to think of the questions in a quick moment, without having to write.)

Quick. No solutions, no explanations, no potential reasons. *Only* questions. Write as fast as you can. No question should be ruled out as too . . . anything. Every question is a spark that takes you somewhere else. Fast. Lickety-split . . . three, five, ten minutes. Just every wondering thought that can come to you. Then, let it rest. Walk away. Put your thoughts on something else, if you have time. And the next day, treat yourself to the same issue and ask more questions.

Several things occur. Patterns develop. And you can see that your inquiry might be weighted toward one general direction. Once you see that, try to head the other directions in your questioning. Again. Walk away. Let the questions settle in.

When you have a couple of sets of questions on a single matter, take a studious look at them. Begin to make assessments. Learn if the questions relate to internal or external structures, to judgments based within yourself or concerns for the opinions of others. Are the questions a matter of education, or are they philosophical or reflective in nature?

Yes. I told you it's like peeling layers off an onion. You end up asking questions about the questions. And in a very interesting fashion—one that will ultimately be unique to you—the process, which you develop in your own style, ultimately heads you to a resolution or creates an answer. Or not. Even without an answer, you will have come to know the issue you are facing in a better way. That's how you get to know anybody. You meet someone, you ask them questions. I can think of several people who have made an incredible first impression on me because they asked such interesting and insightful questions. Not just the "What do you do for a living?" kinds of questions.

 Incite all your own questions—start an idea riot.

Many companies these days are producing tabletop questions—questions in various forms and packaging that are supposed to prompt conversation . . . around the meal table or in the living room. What are some of the most insightful questions you have ever been asked? What would your tabletop question box be like, if you made one for your own use? You can use index cards, cover stock, cut-up greeting cards you've been saving for "something." Write or type the questions. Use your question box as a writing prompt. Share it with your friends. Your family. Use it when you are working through issues and challenges.

as you walk

Endurance

noun. 1. the fact or power of enduring an unpleasant or difficult process or situation without giving way. 2. the capacity of something to last or to withstand wear and tear.

I am in earnest—I will not equivocate—I will not excuse—I will not retreat a single inch—and I will be heard!

—William Lloyd Garrison

even from the darkest night songs of beauty can be born.

—mar

Was I tempted to make an exception to the public transportation plan for this trip? Yes. But I stuck with my intention. I was committed to public transportation and trying to see the divine in each person I encountered. So then it was off to a bus. And another bus. And transfer to one more bus. By then I was hoping my friend Terry's recommendation to see the Dancing Saints mural of St. Gregory's Episcopal Church was a *great* idea. The moment that the fourth bus turned in the direction opposite to St. Gregory's, I just jumped off—no pause, I got off. (How could I have known if I'd just paused a moment I would *not* have had to climb Potrero Hill?) The bus went past me and disappeared going the wrong direction. Just moments later the bus reappeared on its slow haul up the hill. Up. Up. Grinding gears up. Where I wanted to go.

Ditch Potrero—it oughta be called Heart Attack Hill. I thought I was going to die. Unseasonably hot and I was dressed in a suit. The hill was tough, and so was the neighborhood.

Painted cement block apartments. This neighborhood was so tough they wrote the bus information on the asphalt because signs would have been destroyed. This neighborhood was so tough (*How tough was it?*) that—just like the highway worker zone where they double your fine for traffic violations—there were signs bolted, *bolted*, to cement walls, informing you that in this "drug zone . . . all acts of" (followed by a whole list which basically covered selling, soliciting, or using drugs or prostitution) were double the criminal penalty than in any other areas where those crimes might be committed.

Three cars slowed.

One man yelled something unintelligible. It might've been English, I'm not sure. But I was not at risk from these men in cars because all of them, yes, all of them, could be heard laughing at me. Then. The hill. The Dancing Saints church is at the bottom of the *other side of Potrero Hill.* In case I haven't made it clear, the hill was a study in geometric angles. And I was an out-of-shape white girl. The only one in the neighborhood. I walked in the middle of the street. Except for the three cars that slowed and the one guy that yelled at me, there wasn't any traffic. Who drives through such a neighborhood? Oh, yeah. I'm walking through the neighborhood, I thought, so maybe I ought to just stop asking questions.

I was thinking of my friend Terry laughing back on his cool and flat island in Washington. I was convinced he recommend this church as a *joke.*

But I only thought that on the way up the hill. The way down. Geez. Nobody does hills like San Francisco.

I was catching my breath on the first part of the descent. An appropriate word, descent. As in down from a mountain. I was stepping sideways so I didn't just tumble down head over heels. A rough-looking fellow came around the corner just as I let the world's largest yawn fly from my lips. Sound effects and all. He stared at me. I stared at him. I couldn't have been scared if I'd wanted to be. I was too hot: dripping in sweat. My suit coat was tied around my waist. (Four buses earlier it had been cool.) The man was in tattered clothes. He had bloodshot eyes.

Ah. The divine in each person. I remembered. I shrugged my shoulders and gave the guy a crooked smile, and he smiled right back. "Ah tell you what, dawg . . . you in fer some fine sleep a night—you one tired bitch."

"Yes, sir, I am."

"Well, now, you just take it slow, girl. You be fine." He glanced downward. He patted my shoulder and went on his way.

Ah. Divine. The experiment was working so far. Least he called me a tired bitch instead of a fat white girl. It occurred to me that "bitch" and "dawg" are actually affectionate terms. I continued sideways down the hill.

The church building looked like something out of a movie, I thought to myself. I later found out that it is . . . based on something from a sci-fi flick, *Ran*. The rectors were a couple of movie buffs. Large doors. Yep. They were all locked. A little bit Dorothy at the gates of Oz. Fortunately I read the message board and learned I had ten minutes left before the office closed. Ten minutes. I tell you what, dawg. . . .

Jamie was delighted to give me a tour. I so enjoyed myself. A heady odor was in the air. I asked and learned it was from the Anchor Brewing Company just across the way. The smell of ale and the Dancing Saints.

And it was all worth it. Everest in the drug zone and all. I'm glad I stuck to it. Actually, as I tilted my head to the murals circling the church rotunda, I thought of the many hardships they had all endured. I thought of the Continental Army that first winter with George marching all night in the snow without shoes, and told myself to quit my whining. The Dancing Saints were at the end of my journey and had messages for me.

Jamie, my kind tour guide, gave me a cool brochure, which, after yet another bus ride, I read at an Irish pub south of Market, while sucking down a cool Guinness. Thinking of the stuff that makes the saints dance. That boldness of endurance which is the underline to almost every success I can think of.

• tool kit •

A stop watch. An hourglass. The timer set on your cell phone. Give yourself a period of time to "hold on a little longer" on a project of any sort. Endurance isn't always measured in short time frames, but sometimes just a few extra minutes can make a big difference.

Leadership

noun. 1. the action of leading a group of people or an organization. 2. the state or position of being a leader. 3. the ability to lead skillfully.

You cannot be a leader, and ask other people to follow you, unless you are willing to follow, too.

—Sam Rayburn

---

great leadership is not the visit of an unexpected fate but rather a flame which is kept burning in spite of the winds of risk and opposition.

—mar

Although my father provided an excellent model of what leadership could be . . . I was still rather confused about leadership in relation to my own daily practice. At the core of his leadership model was a simple commitment to achieving the goal. Whatever that looked like. For a long time I simply could have called my style "me-doer-ship" rather than leadership. I acted as though real leadership meant that I had to do everything. And be good at it, too! Which meant a willingness to do other people's parts if they didn't want to carry their weight.

Then there was the period of time when I thought leadership meant telling everyone else how things must/should/ought to be done. Somewhere I got the mistaken notion that if a process is the best practice for me, it becomes the best practice for everyone. Oops. Amend that to BIG oops. The phrase "best practices" became a popular shibboleth in the professional world for a while. At this, perhaps the most effective leaders smiled tolerantly.

Leadership at its most effective stance is able to determine an ultimate desired outcome . . . and draws the best practices out of the people responsible for working toward that outcome. The best leaders will redefine the outcome based upon the discoveries in the practices of the people.

As Antoine de Saint-Exupéry observed, "If you want to build a ship, don't herd people together to collect wood and don't assign them tasks and work, but rather teach them to long for the endless immensity of the sea."

John Adams struggled with the "me-do-it" view of leadership, and yet managed to leave a legacy of profound leadership and impact. In two terms as vice president and a term as president, and throughout his life, he struggled and he found a way through. He inspired others to the ultimate outcome of the flame of liberty. As a leader he demonstrated the practice of identifying an outcome and allowing the diversity of his ranks to come to their own best practices. He came to respect a one-time adversary who didn't follow John Adams's protocols but was inspired by his leadership.

On July 2, 1776, after the resolution was passed to issue the Declaration of Independence . . . John Adams returned to his room. Perhaps he had the sense that there would be forty-eight hours of nasty argument over the "slave paragraph" and various other edits, which, in some cases, would improve and clarify Jefferson's brilliant writing—but mostly meant a set of politicians trying to touch and fuss over what they had not crafted. Considering that each man of the Continental Congress was committing treason, Adams would not begrudge them their fussing.

That night he wrote in his journal . . . believing it was the second of July that America would remember for all time.

Privately John mused that *this* would become the holiday of the whole of these United States. A holiday celebrated with "all honor, and seriousness by pomp and grandeur, by parades, by the games of children and the gatherings of family, by the ringing of bells and by the spectacle of illuminations from one end of this grand country to the other."

On the second of July, John Dickenson, believing adamantly in the need to reconcile to Britain, had stepped away from the hall during the vote. Dickenson knew such a vote had to be unanimous, and he was unable to go against his conscience.

On the third of July, Adams foresaw that these united states would long rage in conflict and would never forgive the Congress if they did not free Americans, *all* Americans . . . there must be *no* slavery. We know how far he got with that argument. On that day he warned of a civil war if his associates could not overlook their economic interests for a greater moral vision. He and Abigail never owned a slave. They lived their leadership. When a final scripted version of all the changes had been made, it was absent John Dickenson's signature. Dickenson, within the season, had signed up as a fighting man in the militia. Dickenson shouldered his musket and went out to fight on behalf of the country, which, as he said, was "like sailing into the worst sea on a skiff made of paper."

Yes, what a skiff of paper this country is. We benefit every day from those men and women who pledged their belongings, their sacred honors, and their lives that we may live in the most remarkable ongoing experiment of democracy. That is leadership with legs.

I love the spirit of this country and wish its heart to be rekindled under our vision, with leaders who may be inspired by the heart, the valor, and the vision of John Adams and John Dickenson. John Adams, the man who, in all practical terms, is the structural "father" of our country and, ultimately, the model of a profound leader. John Dickenson, who demonstrated leadership by action toward the greater good, even when at conflict with his personal views.

· tool kit ·

 because
a mantle of leadership is
not too heavy when it's worn
with love and kept with vision;

because you rise above
challenges and allow your
rewards to come bountifully;

because you share rather than
secret away;

because you lead rather than push;

because you imagine and implement,
dream and do;

because of these things (and myriad others)
your success will shine as a light of hope
and inspire numbers you cannot total.

Can you be clear on the outcomes you are expecting of yourself and asking of others? How can you lead while allowing them a vision of their own? Can you create a sense of urgency for them to participate in their most effective way?

may angels
gather at
your shoulder

Belief

noun. 1. acceptance that a statement is true or that
something exists. 2. something one accepts as true or real;
a firmly held opinion.

*The truth is, no one really believes in immortality.
Belief must mean something more than desire or hope.*

—Clarence Darrow

---

*i recognize the delivery of grace to my day, even if i
cannot identify a specific return address.*

—mar

I have lived with the sense of gratitude that the Creator of the Universe hears my voice when I speak, and acknowledges me when I provide an address, a hello, an overture of any sort. I am careful in this, for I recognize that the enormity of G—'s divinity exceeds my capacity to truly name. We come to a sense of holiness in different ways. It is with relief I acknowledge that it is not my responsibility to assess those other ways and roads. I can only know my own. And I rarely name it to any other.

Belief fuels our decisions—even when we are not clearly aware of those beliefs. So, the greater intimacy we have with our own convictions, the greater clarity we have as to how they motivate and direct the actions and attitudes of our life—and the more naturally our actions spring from our beliefs.

Our culture provides a harsh bench upon which it invites belief to sit. People are accustomed to asking, "What *are* you?" As if it is simple to understand a person's spiritual being by affixing a title or category to it. Often the inquiry is really based on a need for comfort. The question could be phrased, "Are you like me? Do you share my beliefs? Is what I believe validated in you by the way you believe?"

But belief transcends ritual, structure, and societal expectation. It is an enlivening, intensely personal core to our being. Our way of being.

There is writing advice that transfers well into the realm of beliefs. The advice is, "Don't tell, show." Many disciplines around the globe advocate that belief should be demonstrated rather than discussed or dissected.

oh divine,
oh sweet core of holiness which dwells within me . . .
may i simply be certain of you.
i don't even have to see you. . . .
i just need to breathe and remember the possibility of you.

holiness which masquerades as hope. . . .
a brilliant and small flower blooming in the snow. . . .

bloom in this, my season of tears.

grace pours from my lips as water over the falls: when i
     speak with
gratitude. the grace of thankfulness.
let me thank you:
for my breath.
for the plenty and abundance i know in my life and
     experience in my thoughts.
in fact . . . THANK YOU FOR . . . seems pettiness as i
     consider the vastness of source.

it is simply enough, isn't it, to be bowed and whisper . . .
     thank you . . . thank you . . .

What beliefs do you hold that are uniquely your own? How much of what you hold as belief have you simply stepped into from your life experiences, your family, your culture? In what ways do your fundamental beliefs impact you on a daily basis? If you're not aware of holding it . . . can it still be called a belief? Who stands in your world as a model of manifesting their beliefs through their actions?

Compassion

noun. sympathetic pity and concern for the sufferings or misfortunes of others.

We are all in the gutter but some of us are looking at the stars.

—Oscar Wilde

---

there is no small act of kindness. every compassionate act makes large the world.

—mar

I was settled in for the long bus ride home. An apparently challenged man sat next to me. He smelled first of vanilla pipe smoke. It quickly occurred to me that scent masked another odor, less desirable! He seemed "in a fog" and, ironically, he immediately started speaking of . . . the fog.

"Do you think it's warm downtown?"

I had just come from downtown. I could answer with certainty, "Yes, it is. About ten degrees warmer."

"And, no fog? You are pretty sure there's no fog downtown, right?"

"Yeh. I'm pretty sure."

"Man. Man. I just can't get used to this fog."

"You just move here?" I thought he was new to the area and still adjusting.

"Nah. I been here for years. But still, I just. . . ." His voice trailed off. I looked out the window. I knew the irony of a long-time resident not being able to get used to a consistent weather condition should be humorous. But I found myself annoyed. I watched the buildings pass by, took note of four different languages on signs in one block, and pondered. How is it that one rails against that which is nearly a certainty? The fog rolling in to the outer Richmond district, off the sea, is as predictable as—well, it's pretty predictable. Is discussing this antagonistic relationship with fog just a shy person's way of interacting with strangers? No. This guy's really troubled by the fog. I think I've just experienced what Marcus Aurelius, in his *Meditations,* called working against the logos, the way of things. I've started thinking of it as "the way of the way of things." Like the epistemology of the life force.

The vanilla-pipe-smell gentleman offered several other observations. He was snuggled in close to me, and I was trying to not be repulsed by his proximity. Note to self: You are trying to see the divine in everyone. Remember?

I looked out the window and remembered the night before. I'd taken the only seat on my bus ride from the same stop. I remembered a man who appeared to be in his late twenties. He was in a drugged haze, slumped forward. Book-ending the empty seat was a gray-haired lady, clutching her bag as if the drug-impacted man would, at any moment, sober up and grab it from her. She fluctuated between looking conspiratorially at me—implying that, since we were the only two people on the entire double bus of a pale skin color, we had to judge together—and glancing at the slumped fellow with disapproval and disgust. I sat down. To her humph. Like a sunflower gently sliding to the sun, this lad began his slow curve around to my shoulder. Before he weighted himself there I looked to his hands. They were empty and relaxed. Pockets? Flat. I sensed I was in no immediate danger.

The next stop brought standing-room-only passengers. One gentleman stood in front of me and my travel companion. He looked at us both, silently assessing. He looked at the boy with concern, so I quietly said,

"Lad, lad, you okay?"

He roused to utter some euphoric, unintelligible phrases, and set his head back squarely on my shoulder. I leaned my neck away so he'd have full berth . . . and just rode along. The passengers who watched all this registered approval, except the gray-haired lady, who managed to sniff out, "It used to be safe to ride the Muni at night."

I wondered when that might have been. When is anything characteristically safe in any large city at night? One of the passengers in front of me, looking down on me, crinkled his features and whispered, "Very nice of you. He's harmless." I wrinkled my nose back and softly nodded in agreement.

As the bus passed further into the Richmond district, there were more empty seats than people. I leaned into the fellow and sat him upright. I moved to an empty seat. Periodically another younger man and I exchanged glances and looked at the passed-out passenger. Finally I said, "I wish I could sleep like that."

"I think his sleep had a little help."

"Yes. Just a little." We chuckled. The bus motored on, and then there were three. The sleeper, the driver, and me.

"Last stop. Point Lobos," the automated system announced.

"Thanks for the ride. Um." I gestured to the single remaining body. "You fine with your last rider?" But what would I do? Help her haul him off the bus? Call somebody? She had a cell phone. It was just an acknowledgment of some sort. And I was glad I made it.

"Thanks," she responded, with chuckling surprise. "I'll take him where he goes." It's nice to find kindness.

Stirring me from my reverie of the bus ride the night before, vanilla-pipe man was explaining the large fireplace he has at his home—for burning things, so he can pretend it's winter, he explained. I glanced outside. There wasn't a lot of pretending involved. This day it really was unseasonably cold.

He said more things to me. I cannot remember what they were. I was busy chastising myself. This week was supposed to be my grand experiment. My opportunity to explore that frequently used term, *namasté*. It is supposed to mean "that which is divine in me recognizes that which is divine in you." I wanted to try that each day. See if I could learn something to take home with me. I was chastising myself that the divine I was able to see in the fogged-out young man the night before did not extend beyond the odor of the man who couldn't get used to fog. My self-recriminations were broken by vanilla man saying good-bye.

"Thanks for your stories," I said to him.

He gently pinched my shoulder and whispered, "Happiness."

Happiness. His divine to mine. Happiness. I wondered what gift, what fire he might have kindled for me, this man who pretends it's winter with his fireplace, if I had kept to my promise of letting the divine in me recognize the divine in another. I was inattentive, given to my own thoughts. Did I miss the opportunity to speak to an angel disguised as a cold, fog-resistant, ruddy man? I'll never be able to know. But I do know this: It takes discipline and compassion to awaken the divine in ourselves long enough to recognize the divine in another. It's too easy to let our spirits sleep, especially on a crowded bus next to a man smelling of vanilla pipe smoke.

Compassion: It's going to take a lot of practice.

· tool kit ·

What has compassion looked like when it was extended to you? What actions lead you to believe someone is compassionate? Is it enough to feel compassion or does true compassion prompt action?

may you know
angels stand
with you
as you rest

Rest

verb. 1. cease work or movement in order to relax, refresh oneself, or recover strength. 2. allow to be inactive in order to regain strength, health, or energy.

Rest is not idleness, and to lie sometimes on the grass on a summer day listening to the murmur of water, or watching the clouds float across the sky, is hardly a waste of time.

—Sir John Lubbock

all that i need is within me. it is poured out freely with a wise hand in appropriate measure. and it is held by the hand of contentment, in rest, that i may be refreshed and greet another opportunity with joy and welcome.

—mar

Some days I feel infinite possibilities, and other days I feel like infinitely napping. But possibility continues to win out. I wish you success in your most important things—and contentment, at least, in everything else.

Success in many settings seems to be measured by how high someone's stress meter rises or how much they have to do. Ask someone how they are doing, as they're bustling about, busy with lists and errands and endless things that "must" be done, and most commonly the answer is an exasperated, "I'm *fine*, but *so* busy!"

Imagine this. Imagine someone in the midst of an office or bustling mall or parent meeting or any other place where busy and important people gather. Now imagine asking this person, "How are you?" and having them answer, "I'm rested. I'm doing what I love doing, but I don't feel stressed about it. And if I don't complete all the things I want to do, at least I know I've given my best effort. And I'm certain to make time for a nap this afternoon."

I don't know. I can just imagine someone sarcastically saying, "Man, I want your life." But they probably don't.

We each must determine what actions we allow to define us. Determine us. Or if we allow actions to do that at all. How do you allow yourself to be defined? And what kind of answers do you provide when people ask you how you are?

Being well rested is a key to a strong immune system and good judgment. Yet rest time is shaved off for hosts of things, not the least of which is television. Ernest Hemingway (who was not a particularly good role model at the end of his life, but had a lot of very good observations) said, "I still need more healthy rest in order to work at my best. My health is the main capital I have and I want to administer it intelligently." For some folks, rest can only be justified by the results in produces in other areas. More energy to *do* things.

Even though naps are a favorite thing, real rest does not comes easily to me. I am bound up with the enormity of what I long to accomplish. It used to take getting sick to make me rest. ("Whaddaya mean 'used to'?" my conscience is asking me.) Pushing myself beyond healthy limits could be considered a hobby of mine. I'm not proud of it, and I did not even want to tell you this. But. It's true. I aspire to "read the signs" along my own roads that are clear indicators that it's time to not only slow down, but to rest. To restore and refresh.

For me, beyond the yummy world of an afternoon nap (which does wonders for me), rest is a state of mind. There's a common slang phrase, "give it a rest, will ya?"

Yes. Give it a rest. Set the weights down. You can pick everything up whenever you want. Just a small rest. Rest begins as a commitment to a way of thinking, and then it moves into the physical world of literal rest.

• tool kit •

What does rest look like for you? Is it a frame of mind? A pause? A nap? Time away? Is rest valid on its own, or does it need to be part of something larger? What answer will you provide today when someone asks you, "How are you?"

Self-Care

noun. regard for one's own well-being and happiness.

If I'd known I was going to live this long, I'd have taken better care of myself.

—Eubie Blake (attributed)

---

sing of your singularity and bask in the shine of all that you are and all that you may become.

—mar

The following is an invitation I wrote to myself for greater self-care in the coming year. It was my celebration of New Year's Eve. The aspirations listed here continue to be important to me as I seek greater ways of loving myself and providing my whole being with the best possible care.

Sanctuary. I assert to all and no one in particular that I need a sanctuary, a restful domicile. Not to simply rest well, but to imagine, create, restore, and envision.

Truth. This year I will tell the truth as well as I am able in all circumstances. The truth as well as I am able to see it. I will rein my words in carefully, and perhaps this year I will learn to listen better than I have.

Nourishment. Awakening early, I will begin my days following my breath and then inviting my body to a greater level of performance. I will feed my system with food that will fuel it well and stimulate my spirit, thought, and body's performance to higher levels of service. In this year I do not want to take false satisfaction from food products but extract my true nutrition from the life of my spirit. I will drink clean and pure water. I will strengthen my muscles for greater endurance.

Moderation. I will not be rigid in my gentle moderation of these longings as they become habit.

Growth. I will continue to celebrate my increasing ability to demonstrate love for myself and others. I will reach in all ways I know, and be willing to discover new ways, for a greater ability to serve myself and others.

I will reach for extraordinary creative expression and work and play to create work that inspires and motivates myself and others. I will rest.

Work. I will celebrate the broadening and expansion of my own body of work. I will enjoy opening doors and celebrating creative and business opportunities for me and my circle of friends.

Friendship. Carefully I will tend the spirits of friends who compose my small circle of friendships. I will do this with mindfulness and purposeful, dedicated time.

Security. I will enjoy broadening the stability of my financial base and will continue movement into stable growth.

Nature. I will learn by name the trees that stand in my world and so diligently help me breathe. I will question and study to understand the soil and have easy conversation with the growing things. I will become aware of the calls of winged creatures. I will notice the patterns of the weather and listen for the messages of the wind.

Learning. I will call my associates to greater use of their own gifts, and I will practice the new disciplines which I am calling forth from myself with joy and privilege.

I will continue to be a student and a teacher.

I will continue to sing my song and be blessed with the music of others.

I will exert discretion in my circle and be conscientious as to who gets to stand close to my heart.

I will inhale and exhale mindfully: I will be grateful for that breath and will work to make certain that I may assist in protecting the breath of others.

I will learn to rest and practice being silly. At least a little silly.

I will dance a little more.

In all ways I will endeavor to be better, smarter, and more true at the end of any day than I was at the beginning. And I will turn to this (year) (day) (week) (month) just turning new and say, "Welcome . . . I am ready for you."

· **tool kit** ·

What are the invitations you can offer to yourself to demonstrate a greater sense of loving toward yourself? How can you begin to both be more gentle with yourself and create a more truthful accountability?

Can you be parent and child, both?

may all your
endeavors be
rooted in
contentment

Comfort

noun. 1. a state of physical ease and freedom from pain or
constraint. 2. (plural) things that contribute to physical
ease and well-being. 3. consolation for grief or anxiety,
reassurance.

*Make friends with the angels, who though invisible are
always with you. Often invoke them, constantly praise
them, and make good use of their help and assistance
in all your temporal and spiritual affairs.*

—St. Francis de Sales

---

*may a thread of comfort be woven through your
difficult days.*

—mar

"A state of physical ease." This applies at a host of levels. In the physical, it can apply to the body as well as to the environment. Much is made over organized and orderly environments in today's home shows and magazines. What element of an environment offers comfort? Where is a place of freedom from pain or constraint?

The word "comfort" is paired, often without thought, with food. I want to pair the word comfort with home. Comfort home. The environment from which you launch yourself into your daily activities, and to which you return for nurture and rest, should be a comfort. An environment which contributes to your well-being promotes ease and a sense of real comfort.

Virginia Woolf wrote of the angel that sits on the shoulder of a creative person reminding them of all the things which must be completed. In my home, I try to give that angel regular time off and invite the angels of comfort and ease in.

There is a way to create a physical environment of comfort. It is different for everyone, and it means that you have to pay attention to the elements which bring you peace, the things that lift the daily anxieties from your shoulders.

A client told me of friends who have a "gathering hall" in their home. It is only used for the frequent gatherings they have with their many friends, and for events they host which support activities that are meaningful to them. She expressed that all she has to do is walk into the gathering room and she feels an immediate comfort and ease. Everything about the room is designed to promote connection and a sense of community.

From the lighting to the furniture to the decorations, the room itself is a fundamental comfort . . . and then the activities that take place in it create the memory of comfort.

Then there's comfort at the level of exchange. It is what we do for our friends in the daily exchanges of our lives. In our best moments, we offer each other perspective, hope, and some laughter over the various anxieties we face. The friend who is anxiety-ridden and quick to point out the things that might go wrong is not the first one we call when we need comfort. That call goes out to the friend who knows how to listen, and whose consistence draws us back up.

There is the level of comfort we offer ourselves. The inner dialogue that we wage when times are harsh. I know one of the things I do when I am seeking a sense of comfort is climb into my most comfortable pajamas, wrap myself in a blanket, and settle in with a fine book. This has been a comforting action to me since I was a little girl.

• tool kit •

What are the things that you do to bring comfort into your home? Who are the comforting people in your life? How is it that you offer comfort to others? Is it different for each circumstance, or always the same?

Observation

noun. 1. the action or process of observing something or someone carefully or in order to gain information. 2. the ability to notice things, esp. significant details.

In a dark time, the eye begins to see.

—Theodore Roethke

---

remember the difference between looking and seeing.

—mar

Just wait. Just wait!

This is one of the most difficult instructions I ever offer to myself. Wait and observe. Observe. Don't interject, interfere, participate, or comment. Just watch and see what happens.

Years ago I enjoyed the consistent conversation of a bookish curmudgeon. When I first started my company, he was skeptical that anybody was going to want to invest in poetry and art beyond birthday cards. But he said he was willing to observe the process and offer his comments along the way. Which he did until he inconvenienced the many of us who enjoyed his crusty ways by dying.

This isn't the point I wanted you to know, but it is an observation, and it's pretty funny. And maybe it is part of the point. The curmudgeon was decades older than me. And one day I specifically asked him if he'd make observations to me about the writing life from the perspective of his age. He obliged with something completely unexpected.

"Watch your knees, they're the first to go. And take extra good care of your teeth." Only as I've aged have I begun to understand what in the world that advice had to do with my writing life.

In another conversation, about an individual's ability to make a difference, we differed on the value of daily reading of key national news sources. Unable to act on everything I read, I objected, "There's only so much I can do. It's so frustrating to be a non-participating observer."

Here's what he pointed out to me. He asserted that if I was an observer, I *was* a participant. He then spoke a phrase that has stayed with me long: "Knowing is doing."

Observation is an action, and a very important one. Observation informs and instructs. Observation allows patterns to be identified. It creates an informational base from which solid decisions can be made.

Rather than the busy-ness of demonstrating how much I know, I can boldly practice observation and learn what others know.

• tool kit •

Keep a log of any issue or action that you want to change. If it's weight loss, log everything you eat. If it's project management or priority evaluation, keep a time log. If you experience injuries from physical activity, keep an exercise log. By carefully observing your habits and patterns, you will begin to see . . . what you need to know.

may all your
endeavors be
rooted in peace

Connect

verb. 1. bring together or into contact so that a real or notional link is established. 2. join together so as to provide access and communication. 3. associate or relate in some respect. 4. think of as being linked or related. 5. (of a thing) provide or have a link or relationship with. 6. form a relationship or feel an affinity.

> *A friend is (a) person with whom I may be sincere.*
> *Before him, I may think aloud.*
>
> —Ralph Waldo Emerson

> *when i want to see friendship defined, i look at you.*
>
> —mar

Riding the bus can be such a vibrant experience with so much to see. Every street is a different snapshot of events and life. Once, when I was a few seats back from the bus driver, an elderly gentleman stepped on, paid his fare, and sat in one of the first seats. At first glance I thought he must be hot, wearing a long-sleeved shirt on such a warm day. But as my eyes focused on the images, I realized he actually had a sleeveless shirt on, and his arms and sternum were covered with tattoos.

A youngster sat across the aisle from him and had the audacity—for which I was longing—to ask him, "Mister, what's that you got all over you?"

He laughed. His answer was kind and rehearsed. Perhaps he had stopped counting the numbers of times he had been asked this question. "Well, you are pretty young, but I know you got friends." The youngster readily agreed. "And maybe one of those friends you had moved away or went to a different school or something, and you might have said to them you would never forget them. You'd always remember them. You ever done that?"

Again, participative agreement from that youngster. Me too.

"Here's the thing with me. When I was just a little older than you, I decided when I really wanted to remember a friend of mine, somebody that I was powerfully connected to . . . I'd just wear 'em. Right on my skin. Then for sure they'd be with me wherever I went, and no way could I forget them. They're on my skin."

Sure enough, I wasn't the only passenger enthralled by the story. Several heads were leaned forward for a closer look. Lots of different styles. But every tattoo was the name, mostly first names, of someone with whom this man had a connection in his life. Accommodatingly, he held his arm out in front of him so anybody that wanted to could get a better look.

He turned his forearm over and pointed out a name, saying, "This 'n here. My first. I was just a bit older'n you. He ain't here no more. I mean, not living anymore. But he lives with me as long as I'm walking. At least."

The bell drew a number of us back to our place in the world. The man with the names tattooed drew up the satchel he had at his feet and said, "Gotta go. Thanks for asking. Remember your friends."

My stop was just a few blocks later. My head was full. As a lettering artist, I found that the many different styles with which that man had decorated himself were writing themselves into my thoughts. Bold. Playful. Stately. Elaborate. I knew without having to ask that the man chose a style that suited the connection he was memorializing.

Not given to tattoo work for myself, yet taken with the intent, I wondered how I might remember this man's efforts in my own life. With my own connections. So much buzz happens around the importance of networking and creating connections. There are ways we indelibly write our names on others without a literal mark. And they on us.

· 176 ·

That day I made connections by not averting my eyes or attention from a youngster and an old man. I do not know their names. I do not know where they live or if they still live. But I am connected to them in an indelible way.

• tool kit •

Connect at a time when you typically disconnect. Sit next to someone you don't know. Speak to strangers in public places. In a meeting, do not go to your usual table, but sit somewhere new. Connect. Make a habit of giving your calling card. That is, a calling card, personal to you. I didn't say business card. It may actually *be* your business card . . . but consider it a calling card that encompasses all aspects of your life. A business card isn't always the most appropriate mechanism for making a connection.

generosity

noun. the quality of being
kind and generous.

*At times our own light goes out and is rekindled by a
spark from another person.*

—Unknown

_____

*the most certain way to realize our own dreams is to
help others realize theirs.*

—mar

In line at the airport coffee stand, a white-shirted Southwest Airlines person, with a tag which simply read "crew," ran and hopped into line behind me. Yes, hopped. I said, "Are you enthusiastic or just in a hurry?"

He laughed and said, "Both!"

"Since you're in a hurry and I'm not, please enjoy being in line in front of me."

"Serious?"

"Yes."

"Wow. Thanks. You just helped a lot of people."

We enjoyed conversation about all sorts of things. Then he ordered. Three regular coffees and three mochas. He took the three coffees right away and rounded the "pick up your order here" corner and began waiting. He tried to get the attention of the barista who was jammed with orders.

"Want me to tell him you'll be back to pick up the mochas?" Relieved, he hopped off. The barista had a line full of people ordering the most complex drinks and seemed to be out of everything he needed. I finally got his attention and told him the three-mocha man would be right back for his drinks. He winced. Right back wasn't going to see those drinks done.

Pretty soon the Southwest white shirt came sprinting back. I delivered the apparent news. It was going to be a while.

"Well, I was able to tell my passengers that with the tailwind we'll have, even with a ten-minute delayed departure, we'll still arrive in San Diego five minutes early. I just told them my crew drinks ordinary coffee all the time, and I wanted to give them something special. Everybody seemed willing to cooperate with that."

"You're the pilot?" I asked, my incredulity not masked.

"I would never keep a plane on a runway if I thought it would make us late . . . but we really do have a following wind. We would have just sat on the runway in San Diego waiting for a way in. So, they'll sit here while I'm getting my crew their coffee."

I turned to the barista and asked how often he had a pilot hold a plane so the crew could enjoy his fabulous coffee. He looked appreciatively at the pilot. "You won't have to keep them waiting much longer." I translated that look to mean he probably serves plenty of pilots in a hurry, but not so many with this cheerful attitude who are buying coffee for their crew. The barista went right to work on those mochas.

"There are all kinds of reasons why I love flying Southwest. This is just one of the best examples. You are all so good to each other, so real—so human. I really appreciate that."

He blushed. And he was saved from responding by the barista announcing, like an athlete crossing the finish line, "Done!" The pilot went sprinting off to his plane.

President Clinton has provided a grand model for generosity in his post-presidency. In his book *Giving: How Each of Us Can Change the World*, he demonstrates clearly that one person's generosity, at *any* level, makes a difference. Have you lost someone you love? Do you know a parent who has faced the pain of the death of a child? Bill Clinton's childhood friend, Paul

Leopoulos, and Paul's wife, Linda, were shocked out of their happy family habits by the car accident that took their daughter Thea's life.

Linda and Paul raised themselves up off their grief-bent knees and purposed to redeem their extraordinary loss with extraordinary giving. With the help of friends, the Thea Foundation was created. Thea benefitted tremendously from the arts and the Leopouloses, in honor of their daughter, benefit thousands of young people throughout the state of Arkansas through programs in arts opportunity, competition, training, and scholarships. They continue to transform their grief into giving.

President Clinton ardently tells this story and dozens of others about the profound impact of generosity all over the world.

· tool kit ·

How can you improve the place you are today by generosity? What does it look like when you demonstrate the boldness of unexpected generosity?

Organize

verb. 1. arrange into a structured whole;
order. 2. coordinate the activities of
(a person or group of people) efficiently.

Settle for disorder in the lesser things for the sake of order in the greater things.

—Ed Monahan (attributed)

---

this is not a mess but rather a profound, complex manifestation of a highly organized and brilliant cognitive process.

—mar

I love containers. Containers of any sort. Bins. Baskets. Boxes. Plastic things with lids. Folders. Portfolios. Bags. I believe I am drawn to the sense of organization that comes when I place a thing *in* something. I look at the pictures in women's magazines and make a sound like cartoon character Homer Simpson makes when looking at Duff beer on a shelf. Maybe I drool a little, too. Just a little.

Oh, I think. Oh . . . how very wonderful if I had evenly positioned shelves around my writing room, and they were all filled with the very same decorated box, with each box having a matching label. Oh . . . and then I look around my writing room. . . .

Quick—let me tell you that my spice drawer is clean and orderly. And I have, at times in my life, had my spices labeled on the top as well as the front, and they have been in alphabetical order. At times. Not now. But still, the drawer is clean. And the spices are easily accessible. Let me tell you that I have, at times in my life, folded my socks and my underwear in uniform fashion and put them in the drawer in color groupings. At times. Not now. I could tell you about the consulting group I worked for when I was in my twenties, where I taught a variety of organization skills. Where I taught executives the finest approach to maintaining their planners and personal file systems. Now I'm looking around wondering where my planner book is.

I love containers. Yes. Perhaps because they give a physical sense of organization. Because the commodities within the containers do not necessarily have to be organized, but the appearance of organization still prevails. But what of true organization?

Step aside from the belief that being organized means being all and doing all. That everything is orderly, plans are laid out and followed, and all things are tidy and well behaved. Life gets quite messy and loud, and it doesn't willingly, at times, fit into an organization chart or hierarchal model.

In the classic film *The Wizard of Oz,* the wizard/professor says to the lion, "As for you, my fine friend, you're a victim of disorganized thinking. You are under the unfortunate delusion that simply because you have run away from danger, you have no courage. You are confusing courage with wisdom." *This* is the place where real organization takes place. In the wild of the storm, I am in the quiet of my tent. There is no doubt that an organized physical environment contributes to great numbers of successes—read any book on feng shui. But organization is in the way you look at the things in your world. The view from the inside out.

Organized thinking, things which proceed from an orderly mind, have a great grace. I've seen the people who, in the midst of a chaotic work environment, seem to know which things to do and in what order. The acronym I use is WIMIN: What Is Most Important Now? And I organize my thoughts around the answers to that question. I find these days that when I am engaged in organizing a physical part of my life, it is because there is disorganization in my thinking, and I am trying to work outside in—instead of inside out.

Will you acknowledge that inside organization happening first may make outside organization happen more effectively?

Pick up your goods and materials from one section of your environment, and put them where they belong. Be purposeful in where you set things down. Put them where they belong *now*. Stop what you are doing and put the thing you are done with . . . away. Each thing in the place where it belongs. Create order in your environment, segment by segment. Don't overwhelm yourself by taking on an entire room. Just take one small part at a time.

afterword

To change your life:
start immediately;
do it flamboyantly,
no exceptions.

—William James

Do you wish to live more flamboyantly, more boldly?

Do you long to embrace the qualities and attributes of your life that are already great and make them even greater? What could possibly be stopping you? One small shift toward bold-ness now. And another one tomorrow. Before you know it, living boldly, will be a habit.

How do I do it? I've incorporated ten of my desired bold-nesses into a pattern that keeps my days leaning forward and increasing in their boldness. I'll share the list with you.

ten ways i live boldly

My purposeful days are full of little leanings, not grand lung-ings. In my own aspiration toward growth and becoming the best version of myself (to use a writing metaphor), I just edit a little. Each day. Little edits add up to great changes. They nurture and cultivate the changes I want to make in my life.

1. Begin the day as if it were on purpose: I invite enthusiasm in.
2. Include movement: dance, aerobics, exercises, biking, walking, physical intimacy.
3. Make nutritionally intelligent choices often.
4. Do a bit toward my passion, my great joys, my dream.
5. Do just a bit toward something difficult, a challenge, which might otherwise be put off.
6. Make the moment for at least one quality connection with a good friend: e-mail doesn't count. Write a letter or send a card or call.
7. Introduce a festivity, a celebration, a whimsey, a little silliness: play.
8. Extend an unexpected generosity toward a stranger.
9. Utilize every opportunity to express gratitude to myself and others and the opportunity to say, "I love you."
10. At the end of the day express gratitudes for the abundance, forgive the shortcomings and invite the finest sleep to come.

Is there something you have been longing to change? To realize? To start? To build?

What holds you back? Do you feel you are not bold enough? Begin now to strengthen those qualities within you that can move toward excellence. I would jump up and down, and shout and wave my arms. But this will have to do . . .

Please start. Now. Start now. Don't wait.

Don't wait. There are those of you for whom these words are all you need.

Don't wait. You know exactly what I mean. And you could stop reading right now.

But keep reading, even still.

The finest stationery in the back of your drawer? The china that you have not used in HOW long? The tools you don't let the kids touch? The special occasion stuff that you hardly ever have occasions special enough to use?

Don't wait.

The love you hold in your heart that you KNOW they know so why bother saying it? The kiss, the lingering touch, the hug, the appreciation of your family? Your friends?

Say it.

The dream you've held for so long? The one that you wish for while you are doing the other stuff? The dream that you think you don't have enough money for, aren't yet smart enough to do or do not have the courage to start?

Begin it.

The person you want to meet? The individual you want to praise, congratulate, honor? The friend you want to reconnect with? The person you have waited to apologize to . . . the relationship you ought to rebuild but keep waiting? The messy garage that makes your shoulders go into your earlobes every time you look at it? The fitness program you keep waiting for a more convenient time to begin? The closet that haunts your mornings because it's so crammed full of stuff that you don't use but don't have the guts to give away? The social ill you want to heal?

Don't wait.

Start on your dreams, your impulses, your longings, your special occasions today. Because this IS your moment. You aren't going to be any smarter, more ready, more able or more qualified than you are right now. Right now. Now is the time to start living boldly. The longing for boldness is enough to begin.

Don't wait.

I have a reminder written on my desk, "lovingly courageous actions chosen intentionally." This is the time in my life where I get to live fearlessly. Where I get to stand in the wind of uncertainty and live boldly. Where I get to put the "currency" of my dreams where the "mouth" of my actions are and make my creative life expand and explode. I've looked in the mirror and said, "Don't wait." And I'm not.

I've looked in the mirror and told myself to "LIVE BOLDLY."

And I am.

And may you find the finest path to your own ways of living boldy.

acknowledgments/gratitudes

Virginia Woolf knew it well: A woman must have a "room of one's own" in order to pursue her creative life. Suze and Jonathan . . . for the room you have provided: let my creative life sing your beauty. And, of course, it would be a "room with a view."

I am blessed by the talents lent to this book by several fine writers:

Caroline Sprinkel-Santangelo, Mike Wigal, Noah Singer, Dr. Len Whalen. Thanks to those in my world who don't mind that our personal stories become a matter of public conversation: my sweet husband, David;

my best four-legged friend, Judah, and the family we spent five years getting him ready for, the Hamiltons; friend of my childhood, Jan;

the name fronting this book in the dedication, Connie Fails.

People whose lives I admire and model in these pages:

President Clinton, Michelle Bernhardt, Paul and Linda Leopoulos, Dr. Deanna Davis, Stephanie Streett, Tina and Taylina, Elizabeth, Andy, Carole, Barbara Anne, Amanda, Terry Hershey, and the fine folks at Southwest Airlines. And I would neglect a debt if I did not acknowledge Hugh Prather and Cheri

Huber. Their wise words have been companions of mine for many years.

Jan Johnson, the publisher at Red Wheel/Weiser and Conari Press and my editor and friend. And all the fine associates at Conari Press who unfailingly lend me their professional support and personal joy. Those fine souls who took the time to read my manuscript and lend their endorsements to this set of words.

Those who have entertained my life with their challenge and difficulty, those who see me through the lens of both adversary and adversity . . . I thank you for the profound lessons you have offered me in living my life boldly. While I will not name you, I most certainly will always remember you.

resources

Andrews, Frank. *The Art and Practice of Loving*. NY: Penguin, 1991.

Bernhardt, Michele. http://www.myinnerworld.com.

Buckingham, Marcus, and Donald O. Clifton. *Now, Discover Your Strengths*. NY: Simon & Schuster, 2001.

Clinton, Bill. *Giving: How Each Of Us Can Change The World*. NY: Random House, 2007.

Davis, Deanna. *Living With Intention*. La Vergne, TN: Lightning Source, 2005.

Huber, Cheri. *The Key:And the Name of the Key is Willingness*. Murphys, CA: Keep It Simple Books, 1998.

Johnson, Addie. *Life is Sweet: 333 Ways to Look on the Bright Side and Find the Happiness in Front of You*. San Francisco: Conari Press, 2008.

Kundtz, David. *Quiet Mind: One-Minute Retreats from a Busy World*. San Francisco: Red Wheel, 2003.

Miller, Beth. *The Woman's Book of Resilience: 12 Qualities to Cultivate*. San Francisco: Conari Press, 2005.

Prather, Hugh. *How To Live in the World and Still Be Happy*. San Francisco: Conari Press, 2002.

Thea Foundation. *http://www.thea foundation.org.*

to our readers

Conari Press, an imprint of Red Wheel/Weiser, publishes books on topics ranging from spirituality, personal growth, and relationships to women's issues, parenting, and social issues. Our mission is to publish quality books that will make a difference in people's lives—how we feel about ourselves and how we relate to one another. We value integrity, compassion, and receptivity, both in the books we publish and in the way we do business.

Our readers are our most important resource, and we value your input, suggestions, and ideas about what you would like to see published. Please feel free to contact us, to request our latest book catalog, or to be added to our mailing list.

Conari Press
An imprint of Red Wheel/Weiser, LLC
500 Third Street, Suite 230
San Francisco, CA 94107
www.redwheelweiser.com